Walking at the Speed of Light

WALKING AT THE
speed
of light

REFLECTIONS FOR FOLLOWING
JESUS IN GRIEF AND JOY

CHERYL J. HESER

NASHVILLE

NEW YORK • LONDON • MELBOURNE • VANCOUVER

Walking at the Speed of Light

Reflections for Following Jesus in Grief and Joy

Published in New York, New York, by Morgan James Publishing. Morgan James is a trademark of Morgan James, LLC. www.MorganJamesPublishing.com

The Morgan James Speakers Group can bring authors to your live event. For more information or to book an event visit The Morgan James Speakers Group at www.TheMorganJamesSpeakersGroup.com.

ISBN 9781683508694 paperback
ISBN 9781683508700 eBook
Library of Congress Control Number: 2017918437

Cover Design by:
Megan Whitney
megan@creativeninjadesigns.com

Interior Design by:
Chris Treccani
www.3dogcreative.net

In an effort to support local communities, raise awareness and funds, Morgan James Publishing donates a percentage of all book sales for the life of each book to Habitat for Humanity Peninsula and Greater Williamsburg.

Get involved today! Visit
www.MorganJamesBuilds.com

DEDICATION

To my husband Doug, who saw the star and has always believed in the Light. He is a strong and steady partner in the journey. To my daughter Anne, whose love for her "little brother" and belief are unwavering. She has shared the grief and the healing. And to my dear friend Sue Lueneburg, whose faith in Jesus is inspirational. She is a constant source of light in my life. To them all, I am eternally grateful.

"When you find yourself in the position to help someone, be happy and feel blessed because God is answering that person's prayer through you. Remember: Our purpose on earth is not to get lost in the dark but to be a light to others, so that they may find their way through us."

–ALBERTO CASING

"I firmly believe that in every situation, no matter how difficult, God extends grace greater than the hardship, and strength and peace of mind that can lead us to a place higher than where we were before."

–ANDY GRIFFITH

"What could be more comforting than to fold grief/ like a blanket -- / to fold anger like a blanket,/ with neat corners -- / to put them into a box of words?"

–MARY OLIVER

TABLE OF CONTENTS

FOREWORD

I first met Cheryl Heser in Forsyth, where I pastored the church she attended. She was, and still is, a bright and shining star in this world. She graced me with gifts of her poetry, laughed with me, cried with me, and shared her grace toward the world with me. It was an honor to get to know her.

Cheryl called me when Josh died. She knew that I would understand her pain, as I had lost a son in 2000. From that moment on, Cheryl struggled to find the light in the darkness, to find hope in sorrow, and to find life after death.

Cheryl has become the light in the darkness for many parents who are struggling to survive the loss of a child. She and her family made the decision to donate Josh's organs, a life-giving miracle for several other families. Cheryl is fully engaged in her grief journey, and never hesitates to share her story, and her heart and soul, with others who share her loss.

I never wanted to be a member of "that club" of parents who are grieving the loss of their child, but if I have to walk this walk, I want to do it with Cheryl. The light she seeks shines through her and on all those around her. Josh is alive in her, and his light adds to hers. With Cheryl as a guide and a light-bearer, the journey is just a little bit easier.

And so Cheryl offers her light to you. May it be a blessing, and a gift, and a miracle in your life. Whatever your loss, whatever your darkness, this light will bring you hope and peace and joy. Cheryl, I am honored to be your friend. Thank you for allowing me the privilege of introducing you, and Josh, to the world.

Blessings,

Vicki Waddington

Pastor, Central Montana Parish (4 churches), member of Yellowstone Annual Conference, United Methodist Church, and Yellowstone Presbytery, Presbyterian Church USA. Served on the Montana Suicide Mortality Review Team, teaches junior high classes on suicide prevention and survival, has traveled the State of Montana as a speaker and leader of candlelight services for families who have lost children.

January 2018

INTRODUCTION

A mother and daughter I know well have a syndrome called Seasonal Affective Disorder, a condition based upon light deprivation, especially in winter. Sufferers from this serious disorder deal with depression, difficulty concentrating, withdrawal from others and hopelessness as well as physical problems like lack of appetite. The whole problem is a lack of light. Interestingly enough, artificial light does not satisfy this need; the sufferer needs sunlight.

Granted, most of us are fortunate enough not to have to deal with such a disorder. However, countless people do deal with a similar problem when it comes to spiritual life. Our materialistic society may offer everything we physically and mentally need – almost all of it dependent on electricity, the source of light for everything from living rooms to patios to reading lamps, not to mention computers or cell phone chargers. But amid all the glittering benefits of materialism, we are groping in the dark for some meaning to life, some promise beyond the next thing that money can buy or society can provide. We all need the natural light of God, the light which can only come from the Light of the World.

One aspect of this spiritual disorder is that the symptoms are so similar to the physical disorder. People who experience depression, difficulty concentrating, withdrawal from others, and hopelessness

– plus physical problems as well – can look to the lack of the Light of God.

The purpose of this book is to "shed some light" on this subject very dear to my heart and to offer you some insights which hopefully will open some shades and shutters in your own lives. In every dark moment, Jesus waits for us to look His way, to take the first faltering steps into the light of His presence and to begin or resume our journey walking with Him. I pray that I can glorify Him by offering these words in His service.

In studying Jesus as the Light of the World, I realized that an essential component of our Christian life is to stay in that Light, to walk so closely with Him that darkness cannot claim us.

Because of personal experience, I can tell when I am secure in that Light and when I get out of step and mire down in the shadows of depression and sin which only Jesus can dispel. Now I want to share my thoughts with readers, hoping and praying that His Light will shine through and give meaning to your lives as well.

✦ *PART I* ✦

A STORY OF GRIEF AND GRACE

CHAPTER 1

A Son Named Joshua

The final chapter of my son Josh's life began in an unpredictable accident on a country road. A low tire on the open Bronco edged too close to the edge of a ravine and tumbled the vehicle down while four people were catapulted out. Three of them staggered to their feet and discovered Josh lying inert where the vehicle had rolled over his head. The driver performed CPR while the others begged through cell phones for help, and Josh breathed quietly as an ambulance screamed, a helicopter whisked through black skies, and the emergency staff of Benefis East Hospital whirled into action.

We received the call no parents ever want to experience that night and drove 300 agonizing miles to Great Falls, Montana, arriving just a few hours before our beloved son, only 33 years old, was pronounced brain dead. Our older son and daughter and families arrived, and we clung to each other through that unbelievable day. I sobbed and tried to read since I could not sleep that night. At about 4:30 in the morning, when I finally was dozing, I was awakened by my perpetually early-rising husband and beckoned to a hall window, where he had discovered the sign which would sustain him through the months to come. In the morning sky shone a star with a perfect cross over it.

In a moment's thought I return there. Breathless, we behold the brilliance of the cross manifested in starlight. Like the Christmas star beckoning to shepherds and kings to welcome the Christ, this star welcomes our beloved son into eternity. Interstellar travel bursts on the wings of eagles at the speed of light -- and his death and our lives become transformed. Easter's wooden cross changed from dross to gold shines as brightly as the Christmas star, fulfilling the promise, turning the wise men's rich gifts into the richer gift of salvation.

As my thoughts indicate, we are people of strong Christian faith. Without doubt, we knew from the morning of the star that our son Joshua was in Heaven, safe in the outstretched arms of God, and that we would see him again when we, too, were there in Heaven. However, belief was a tiny boat cresting over wave after wave in a turbulent sea of desperate memories and barreling into troughs of despair. I could not perform as captain, navigator, or even assistant but could only cling to the side and watch Josh's life pass before my eyes.

In 1979 my husband Doug and I had been married five years, had added two children to our family, and had invested in a little ranch in mid-Montana. We were about as "hard up" as people can be, living on close to nothing. Doug labored up to 18 hours a day on our place plus loading hay bales by hand on semi trucks until he ended up hospitalized with serious pneumonia because he could not allow himself the time to take care of himself. Meanwhile, I had taken a job as a nurse's aide at a hospital and nursing home from 4:00 to midnight, working with my husband in the fields while caring for little children all day and then working half the night.

Introduce into that scenario the fact that I had known in my heart for some time that we would have another child, that he would be a boy, and that we would name him Joshua. As a result, discovering that I was pregnant in the midst of difficulties was no surprise. I worried about constant lifting of elderly people and changed jobs to be a dispatcher for the sheriff's office at the same hours, not knowing that the officers were taking turns following me home at midnight because I was obviously fatigued to the point of danger.

The danger increased when I developed toxemia and extremely high blood pressure, forcing me to quit work, rest, and eventually end up hospitalized. The doctors had decided to do a caesarean to deliver my large breech baby when I went into labor and had him naturally. Doug and I had breathless moments when the doctors unwrapped the cord from around our boy's neck and worked with him until he breathed and cried for the first time. Joshua had entered the world. How can a parent express what happens when another life is added to a family, an obvious gift from God? We scrambled and scraped and dealt through tiredness and bliss with a new baby, and all our lives and happiness grew exponentially.

CHAPTER 2

Life and Death

Our big baby boy would grow to be 6 feet 8 inches and 240 pounds, strong beyond description but always the "gentle giant." Josh was our oldest boy Clint's best friend, our daughter Anne's beloved "little brother," and a friend to everyone he met. Troubled souls flocked to him because he was a non-judgmental listener whose concern and humor lightened burdens. Meanwhile, he coped with the challenges of dyslexia and struggled through school, helped by the knowledge that he could constantly win championships in horsemanship with his amazing horse Eagle.

Imagine a graduation day for a young man who had persisted so successfully and now received a surprise "Across America" scholarship to attend diesel mechanics school! Off our country boy went to Phoenix, where he worked loading trucks at night and completed a two-year degree which netted him a job setting up and repairing farm machinery and trucks in central Montana. The company, which had many outlets in our state, gave him its top Efficiency Award, earned because of his care and concern for the many ranchers and farmers for whom he did machinery setup and repairs throughout that part of Montana. The next step was his own shop near the tiny town of Grass Range, Montana, set in the midst of an entirely agricultural area. His success in working for hundreds of grateful patrons was phenomenal. Meanwhile, he married, and although he had no children of his own, he was a favorite uncle for every niece and nephew and a well-loved friend to every other child in his orbit.

Let me paint you a brief picture of this extraordinary young man. Huge in stature, he became formidable when anyone compromised his expectations. At all other times, his mischievous grin and sparkling eyes frankly met those of everyone around him. His friends were myriad, and he could always find someone to go four wheeling or hunting with him as well as barbecuing and "hanging out." Neighbors always invited him and his new horse Tucker to their brandings and cattle trailings. A powerful bow hunter, he felled a bull elk with only one arrow. With a huge pack on his back, he carried supplies for his brother's family as they hiked the backcountry and peaks of the Beartooth Mountains in south central Montana. For his mechanic business, Josh would travel many miles to assist anyone with vehicle and machinery repairs, yet he would interrupt his shop work to teach a little boy how to ride a bike.

A Time of Grief

However, if you think that this book is about my easy acceptance of cataclysmic loss based upon my faith, you are wrong. Grief has been my constant companion ever since October 24, 2013. We are advised of the steps of grief originating with Dr. Elisabeth Kubler-Ross and so amazingly portrayed by Sally Field in *Steel Magnolias*, but what we are not told is that grief is not linear. It circles around over and over like a vicious whirlpool, re-engulfing us, threatening to drown us at the slightest stimulus -- a familiar smell, a treasured song, a friend's smile, a picture, a beloved pet, a rider a-horseback.

The day before Josh's funeral we gathered as family to meet the minister and to view the slide show Anne had created for her brother from birth to present day, accompanied by favorite songs. When it started with "Mommas, Don't Let Your Babies Grow Up to Be Cowboys" and Josh's baby pictures, I collapsed in tears and still do not remember one thing from about five hours of that day. I sincerely believe that Jesus moved me away for those hours before grief could destroy my mind and emotions. The next day I was able to voice Josh's story at his funeral and to share the day with over 640 people who came to say goodbye to him.

A few weeks later, our dear friend Father Tony Schuster came to our town to offer a traditional Catholic graveside service as we buried the small casket with part of Josh's ashes. Father Tony spoke the words which were to inspire so much of my future contemplation during times of grief -- "Eternal rest grant unto him, and may Perpetual Light shine upon him" – and light broke through the clouds of that November day and shone on the casket of ashes. The Perpetual Light of Jesus became not only my vision of Him and Josh in paradise but also my mantra for my own grief journey.

CHAPTER 3

Grief and Resurrection

My mourning continued as my husband obtained Josh's roping horse Tucker, his saddle and his old pickup, all things which assuaged Doug's grief with hands-on experiences. Doug also went outside very early each morning to find a certain star, gaze at its light and talk to Josh. Our son Clint broke down over the loss of his brother and best friend but then sustained himself and his family through their mourning with his strong Christian beliefs and Bible reading. Our daughter Anne shared grief with her children, making collages of Josh's pictures for their rooms, and went a step further. At the bank where she is an officer, her friends and colleagues had witnessed her tears over her "little brother"; in the months to follow they came to her with stories of their reconnections with brothers and other family members, with their realization that precious people in our lives could die at any time. She smiled and cried with them and recognized that Josh's love was extending in all directions.

I watched my family cope and went on living each day, but I didn't heal despite constant prayer and writing. The next step in the saga of grief came when Doug and I went to the funeral home to order Josh's tombstone, deciding on rose granite engraved with his name and dates, a riderless horse and crossed wrenches, and the words "Beloved husband, son, brother, uncle and friend." On December 31, while my husband was at a distant ranch camp feeding cattle, the funeral home director informed me that the tombstone had to be paid for before the new year in order to keep the agreed price. I went to town and paid for the stone, then stopped at the cemetery to visit the gravesite and talk to Josh before I prayed hard for comfort that did not come. That sleepless night I wrote this poem:

RESURRECTION

A little plot of land, surrounded by trees, hills, and sky,
Where the dried grasses are slowly covered with snow
On this frozen day; and my cold, cold heart and eyes
Search for precious ashes buried somewhere deep below.

On this unbelievable day, as an old year fades away,
I bought a rose granite tombstone for my beloved son;
How often have I shared hope, "It isn't carved in stone,"
But this time the hope is gone and the deed is done.

How can my heart beat into a new year he'll never know,
A birthday his jaunty laugh will never celebrate?
How can I find worthwhile life when his life is done,
When a stone and a mother's heart carry such a weight?

In April, sunshine will draw leaves from the surrounding trees
And somehow the snow will yield to a green, abundant lawn.
As spring brings the gift of renewal of nature's living,
Then the plot and the stone will somehow become one.

If dead grasses, browned leaves, and buried seeds return to life,
Resurrection is more than hope – now it is truth to tell.
"Beloved husband, son, brother, uncle and friend" he remains,
Warming this small piece of earth, and hopefully hearts as well.

--C.J. HESER, NEW YEAR'S EVE 2013

This poem is titled "Resurrection" and ends with my belief that "Resurrection is more than hope," but ultimately the poem expresses the grief that brought me to my knees that night. My mother's heart was broken, carrying more weight than I could bear. The idea that it is not natural for parents to bury their children may seem like a cliché until it is experienced. I was in a time-warp, tossed into some unrecognizable progression of events, forced to accept unreality as reality, like some frightened alien landing on a newly-discovered planet. Being out of sync with the people around me paralyzed me at times.

I remember a discussion in a philosophy class in college concerning the Greeks and their striving toward moderation in all things. We students ultimately agreed that although the Greeks had a point, they were also a passionate people, and humankind does not learn passion from moderation. How can we appreciate being really warm unless we experience being really cold? How can we appreciate great joy if we have never known great sadness or grief? Along that line of thinking, how can I share with you my experience and knowledge of walking in the true Light if I do not take you to the place where I knew true darkness?

CHAPTER 4

Walking in Darkness

The darkness in this cavern is now complete. I grope with my hands and senses along cold, unfeeling walls and find not a single chink in the armor of this enemy. My own heartbeat becomes too faint to detect for the reassurance of life-giving blood coursing through my body. If the sensation were only bleakness, perhaps my feet could carry me onward, but the grief tangles with aloneness. I cannot see my way nor can I see others to know if they see the way. The only clear thought in the midst of desperation is that my choices are to end my life or to curl up like a fetus and succumb to the darkness and chill.

Remember the scary stories of youth based on falling into a black hole such as an open grave? The reaction, of course, is to jump and scramble and try every possible way to get out. If people have never experienced true depression, they assume that the jumping and scrambling would be the natural reaction. However, the black hole becomes a sinister "comfort zone," a retreat almost, and those who dwell within it can come to a point where they avoid the light and accept the darkness as reality. I have been there – fortunately not as long as many others simply because my early Christian training instilled in me a resilience which I will deal with in a later chapter.

My heart goes out to those who reside in the black hole long enough to need a major hand up to even think of climbing out.

Unlike those who disparage clinical psychologists – partly because some of them are outspokenly anti-Christian – I believe that great strides have been made in the fields of medicine of all kinds and that we can seek help on different fronts. Some people go through deep analysis and treatments including shock therapy and come out of the hole. Others are given relief with prescription drugs, although because I have seen such disasters with drugs, including antidepressants which make people suicidal and mind-altering drugs which are addictive, the caution flag must go up on that "solution" unless heavily monitored. In studying depression, I seemed to find more disastrous endings than hopeful ones; but I also found evidence that God gives humans abilities to heal in different ways and depression can be cured or at least curbed.

Speaking of God-given gifts, solace can come from people who are good listeners and in tune with our despair and our needs. Some months after Josh's death, I was struggling with some major issues at work. I found myself at the end of a work day staring at my original objective which had not been accomplished. I found myself struggling with focus, disorganizing rather than organizing, floundering rather than charging ahead. Because both of my parents suffered from extreme dementia before they died, I became terrified that at nearly age 66 I was suffering from the initial stages of dementia.

That February my daughter and I scheduled a cruise, something which we thoroughly enjoy together. We flew to Houston, Texas, and got on the ship bound for three ports in the Caribbean. Hours before our scheduled embarkation, a barge collided with an oil tanker in the harbor and because no ships could move before cleanup, we stayed there for four days of our seven-day cruise. A tragedy? No, we were well fed and greatly diverted by the Entertainer of the Year competition, but mostly we talked.

At one point when we were speaking of Josh's death and our grief, my daughter confided that she was really worried about herself because she could not focus at work, found herself unusually disorganized, floundering, and arriving at the end of work days without her initial objectives accomplished. She was 36! I stared at her and then burst into tears. Rather than terrifying dementia, I was suffering from symptoms of grief shared by my much-younger daughter. Although I felt for her and renewed the feeling for myself, the relief provided by the knowledge that I could eventually be okay was beyond description.

Grief and depression grip many people in their sharp claws, and solutions, including the commonly accepted "time heals all wounds," are nebulous at best. We flounder in the darkness. The only real way to bear such a burden is to turn to the Lord who said, "Lay your yoke upon me" and lean upon Him. Every night in my prayers I asked Jesus to hug my son Josh, and then I felt physically hugged as well. Those moments were tiny steps in beginning to walk with Jesus, at the speed of the Light of the World.

CHAPTER 5

Transplants and Miracles

I f the story of Josh ended with my grief and thoughts on eternal life, I would not have written this book. Instead I have to take you back to the moment of Josh's brain death. Josh was an organ donor, and his widow and all his family affirmed his commitment. Eventually, more than 100 people would benefit from six major organs and myriad parts like eye corneas, skin, bone, vertebrae, muscles, tendons, veins and much more. His veins saved two people from amputations, just part of the story of life rescue and enhancement.

Some organs are size specific, which means that very large men who had been waiting for a long time received his heart, liver and lungs. The heart recipient told us that his heart disease was so advanced it had prohibited him and his wife from having children. Now, with Josh's heart beating in his chest, he is the father of a little girl. We were able to meet this remarkable young man, hug him, and hear our son's heart beating through a stethoscope. What an amazing moment!

The story of Josh's organ donation through LifeCenter Northwest, which coordinates the donating and receiving of organs, takes us back to that hospital room where two miracles were happening. The first involved me directly. With his head covered with a white cloth, Josh was lying hooked to a respirator which kept his lungs working and heart beating, sustaining his body warm and "alive." Much of my time was spent holding his huge hand, which was unresponsive but warm and touchable. Miraculously, I felt his strength flowing into me like a healing river, sustaining me, enabling me to deal with his death. To this day I feel that strength.

For the funeral, I wrote this poem which stands framed in each of our family's homes next to a plaster cast of his handprint made by the organ transplant team.

JOSH'S HANDS

These large, strong mechanic's hands,
Darkened by work and a bit of grease,
Still warm, they harbor strength
Even as they lie here in peace.

These hands have worked very hard,
Given hours to each rancher's need,
Gripped the wheel for many, many miles
Where fields needed tilling or seed.

These hands have held his wife so close,
Hugged loved ones with strength and care
Accompanied by his fun-loving grin
And eyes glowing, honest and fair.

These hands have been gentle with horses,
Training them with skill and more,
Using them for cattle work and branding,
Roping, riding, making play out of chore.

These hands were the joy of little children,
Cradling babies, joining tots in play,
Swinging kids, helping them ride bikes,
Making them laugh, lighting their day.

Today as we treasure all his gifts,
Everyone who loved him understands
That all of our lives have been touched
By Josh's dear life and Josh's hands.

--C.J. HESER, NOVEMBER 2013

Second, as Josh lay there, his left lung, slightly damaged when he was thrown from the vehicle, actually miraculously healed to the point that it could be used for a transplant. Can you imagine the body healing in such a way even after the brain no longer functions?! Praise God for the amazing bodies He has created for us! The recipient of Josh's lungs is now living a full life, engaged to be married, and, coincidentally, just retired from running his own mechanics business.

Each letter that we receive, each communication from the donor organization, each attendance at yearly gatherings of organ donor and recipient families, affirms for me that looking toward the future is the best way to deal not only with grief but with all of the trials of life. Of course, not every loved one who dies is going to be an organ donor. But every loved one who dies contains within his or her life something which can move on into the future with us, something which can literally enlighten us.

When my mother died at age 92, her memorial requests were for the Sunday School Department of the church she and my father attended for so many years. A teacher asked that the funds be spent for Bibles for the third and fourth grade classes. When the Bibles were given out, one little boy's reaction was something I knew would have brought joy to my mother's weary heart. Asked why the new books had footprints across the cover, the boy replied, "Because 'Thy Word is a lamp unto my feet and a light unto my path'" (Psalm 119:105). Amen.

✦ *PART II* ✦

LIGHT AND THE
LIGHT OF THE WORLD

CHAPTER 6

Let's Look at Light:

Science Affirms Christian Belief

Getting scientific for a moment, the speed of light is determined to be 671 million miles per hour. Wow! How can we even comprehend that speed? It is like trying to comprehend the national debt! This 671 million mph actually is the maximum speed at which all matter and information in the universe can travel. The main thing we learn from this information is that all travel through the universe is finite – amazingly fast, but finite. But more important, the speed of light interrelates space and time.

What does all of this mean to the person searching for meaning in spiritual life? First, God created the universe and the light -- set in motion all of these mind-boggling things -- and He remains steadily in charge no matter how things change. Astronomers share such things as the fact that the light seen from stars left them many years ago, allowing the study of the history of the universe by looking at distant objects. Second, the correlation of the science of the speed of light and our religious beliefs in the Light of the World brings together science and religion, two parts of our lives and studies which too many people have seen as opposed.

Fortunately, I grew up with my father, a talented lab scientist and college professor and one of the most devoted believers I have ever known. Poppo saw God's hand in every atom and molecule in chemistry and every living thing in botany and zoology. He saw a prayer in a "posy" and all of science as proof of the glorious vision of the Creator. His lack of any problem with natural evolution (other than the notion of mankind evolved from apes) -- based on his observance of the necessity of change throughout the life of the universe -- is another manifestation of the combination of knowledge and faith which lit his life. Poppo would have loved this book.

Kaleidoscope

Light enhancing all humanity of all ages, swirling from the Milky Way and beyond into our existence through stars, moon and planets; sunshine nourishing our lives, pulling from the earth all greenness, the myriad shades and forms of flowers, the creatures living from the plants and bearing young; prisms gathering the light, flashing its beauty to all corners of our darkness; rainbows glowing in refracted loveliness, still shedding tears as the dark clouds dissolve; human faces turned toward brightness like sunflowers, gathering in the power of light no longer diffused by the shades of uncertainty; children dancing in the sunlight, running through sprinklers scattering glowing droplets of water and joy; people strolling on beaches, watching waves sparkling with sunlight, crashing into oceans caressing coral reefs where beams touch multicolored fish swirling around sea fans and anemones; eagles soaring toward the sun, casting brief shadows over sun-bleached prairies and hills as the warmth of another day sheds brightness on their circling forms; beams darting through windows to light inner worlds where souls struggle out of the dusky dungeons of need for affection and answers; dawnlight permeating stained glass until saints let the sun shine through them into our reaching hands and hearts, reflecting the glow of Eden's beckoning paths, the glisten of Christmas, the glorious light of Easter's Christ in the garden; and at the center the fairest face of the Light of the World, the Son of our sunrises and sunsets, the beloved Godlight personified, illuminating today and evermore.

–C.J. HESER, AUGUST 2015

Light has always fascinated me – its essential role in our existence, its beauty, its manifestation in everything from sunrises to sunsets to constellations to comets to rainbows, its connection to warmth and happiness, and its amazing role in the tiniest processes like photosynthesis. I will never match Ansel Adams or Eliot Porter, but from early childhood I have loved the role of light in photography, seeing all of nature and mankind enlightened by the contrast of sun and shadow.

In studying Jesus as the Light of the World, I realized that an essential component of our Christian life is to stay in that Light, to walk so closely with Him that darkness cannot claim us.

Since I have long been dazzled by the study of the speed of light, my revelation was the realization that walking with Jesus is to travel at the speed of Light. Since then, I can tell when I am secure in that Light and when I get out of step and mire down in the shadows of depression and sin which only Jesus can dispel.

CHAPTER 7

Our Need for Light

Christmas Starlight

The western hills seem to reach out tonight
And gather slivers of silver starlight;
Send them shimmering over snowy plain,
Reflecting into the skies again.

The story is told that a Star poured light
Over Judean hills one night
To fill, with whisper of angel wings,
The hearts of shepherds and dreams of kings.

The light shone through them to all mankind --
Light to the people of darkness, the blind,
The poor, the tired, the sinful, the lost,
Warming like fire against the frost.

Dispel our darkness with Starlight, Lord,
To beam out from us in deed and word
To glistening skies filled with song again
Of peace on earth, good will to men.

-C.J. HESER, NOVEMBER 20, 1982

In the introduction, I mentioned Seasonal Affective Disorder, one of the many medical and mental conditions which point to our need for light. When I wrote in this poem of "the blind, the poor, the tired, the sinful, the lost," I touched on some of the life situations which bind us in darkness, in desperate need for Light. If you read of Jesus' life and words in the Gospels, you meet people coping with every one of these conditions. If you open your eyes and ears to your own hometown, you will meet people struggling the same. If you take a real look in the mirror and then widen your gaze to your extended family and friends, again these people will emerge.

Jesus' life on earth should fascinate us all. If God's Son really wanted to reign as Messiah and take this world by storm, wouldn't it make sense for Him to start at the top? He could have taken on the Romans, all the way up to Caesar Augustus, and the Jewish aristocracy, starting with the tyrant Herod. In fact, God could have chosen a royal mother rather than Mary. If we think in terms of the politics of power, why didn't He take that route? The answer is that history proves that method does not work – victory is temporary, and all the emperors and kings, like Keats' Ozymandias, are under the sands. Instead, Jesus chose the blind, the poor, the sinful and the lost for His miracles and the message of His kingdom. You see, people in power assume that they make their own light as evidenced by the unreachable Pharisees and Sadducees, whereas the people Jesus walked among were looking to Him in desperation for light.

People are not the only part of God's creation which needs light, of course. Take a walk with me into my gardens. One is an indigenous garden with native Montana plants all the way from juniper, chokecherry and buffalo berry to golden and brown gallardia (blanket flowers), blue flax, delicate pink wild roses, and dark pink cone flowers. Close by is a rock garden full of perennials, some bearing fruit like currants, sand cherries, elderberries, strawberries and raspberries, some succulents like "old hen and chicks," some herbs like thyme, basil, and sage, and some decorative like golden forsythia, red-bloomed honeysuckle, white snowball bush, lavender lilac, candy-colored pinks, purple climbing clematis and chameleon-like Magic Carpet spirea changing each season. Down the hill is a vegetable garden, prolific with everything from huge pumpkins to slender snow peas, deep-rooted carrots and beets to tall sunflowers and tempting tomatoes.

While we are enjoying the gardens, let's think about the source. Our Creator designed all of this variegated beauty and bounty, every bit of it dependent on light and photosynthesis to survive and flourish. If we scattered all the seeds and cuttings on a table, most of them would be brown and many of them would be indistinguishable unless they are seeds we eat, like peas and corn. Yet buried in God's earth, nourished with water and soil nutrients, each seed and cutting becomes a unique plant which reaches for the light and bears fruit and beauty. What a miracle of life and light!

When God said, "Let there be light," He provided the foundation for the growth of all things, including the people created in His own image to bear His light. Just as plants cannot survive, grow, or prosper without photosynthesis, we cannot do any of those things without the process within us which thrives in the light. Think about us -- variegated people bearing the fruits of the Spirit, living in His light from the moment of conception, loved unconditionally by the Light of the World.

CHAPTER 8

Enlightened Forward Thinking
in the Bible

nto the dark void a powerful voice commands, "Let there be light" (Gen. 1:3). From that point on, each part of the universe and our world is created, from the sun and moon, seas and land, to all living things that dwell on the Earth including man. Isn't it interesting that the light came first and that all other creations of God are either sources of light or dependent upon light? I relish using the word "enlightened" throughout this book because although the modern definition of the word refers to a rational, well-informed view, its roots in Old English mean "to shine." Thus, enlightened believers need not only knowledge and reason but also God's source of light in all being to really shine.

The Word of God is based from Genesis to Revelation on forward thinking. The creation of the world was good in the eyes of the Creator because it reflected His glory and provided a home for mankind. As dismal as being expelled from the Garden of Eden was -- after Adam's and Eve's great sin -- it nevertheless involved God sending them forth into the future, one which will always involve rebellion against Him necessitating reconciliation but also will always involve forward movement both physically and spiritually. The Promised Land beckons, the Messiah beckons, the prophets predict the future at God's direction, and both believers and nonbelievers are propelled into the future which will bring Jesus.

The beautiful rainbow created in the sky after the Flood as a covenant with Noah is one of the greatest manifestations of light and promises for the future given by God to all people. Scientists know how refracted light separates into the multicolored bands of the rainbow, but such knowledge cannot exceed the wonder when we gaze into the sky or a waterfall and drink in that rainbow beauty and the hope promised by our God. My brother recently introduced me to "ice rainbows," light on crystals in the air backlit rather than reflecting the light from behind the viewer like a regular rainbow. Every time I see a new light creation, something internal bounds for joy like a dancer on a spotlighted stage.

When the extraordinary Old Testament woman Ruth says to Naomi, "Wherever you go, I will go," she establishes the lineage of Jesus and moves the salvation of mankind to another level. Don't you love the words of the prophets, those people from Isaiah and Jeremiah to John the Baptist who continually give people hope of the Messiah? My favorite prophet Isaiah wrote the words which inspired my thoughts when we were feeding cattle early one Christmas morning.

Christmas Sunrise

We awaken and chore in prairie darkness,
The hills barely edged with hints of morning.
Slowly the dark clouds pale to blue,
Brushed with strokes of pink and rose.
The eastern sky brightens to gold;
Beams streak west to wake the mountains.
A deer tastes the frost-sprinkled clover,
Sensing as we do the gifts of dawn's gold
And incense of clear air and grasses.

The new day recalls old, precious words:
"The people that walked in darkness
Have seen a great light.
They that dwell in the land of shadows,
Upon them hath the light shined . . . .
For unto us a Child is born,
Unto us a Son is given."
Gently He comes . . . Christmas sunrise.

–C.J. HESER, DECEMBER1983

In speaking of the Old Testament, we know that David described God's Word beautifully as "a light unto my path, a lamp unto my feet" (Psalms 119:105). The glow of that lamp may guide our footsteps, and that is important. But it is not the same thing that Jesus is speaking of when He tells us that He is the Light of the

World. That role bursts into our existence like fireworks, like Roman candles, like volcanic eruptions. No more talk about the soft light!

For those of you who approach this book with caution -- wondering if Christian belief is the antithesis of what you are looking for in the way of strength and direction – I say again: No more talk about the soft light! The answers I have found are powerful, explosive, world-changing. The Zealots who were disappointed because Jesus did not come charging in on a huge warhorse to vanquish the Romans did not realize He was offering something much more powerful and world-changing than just a battle. He is a conqueror of everything mortal, including death itself -- more powerful than the original creation of light!

CHAPTER 9

The Light of the World

No picture of Jesus and our relationship to Him as followers is more prevalent in the New Testament than the concept of Him as the Light of the World. Let's begin with John 8:12: "Again Jesus spoke to them, saying, 'I am the light of the world. Whoever follows me will not walk in darkness, but will have the light of life.'" Jesus was fulfilling Isaiah's prophecy in Isaiah 9:2: "The people that walked in darkness have seen a great light; they that dwell in the land of the shadow of death, upon them hath the light shined." Notice that Isaiah is not speaking just of walking in the dark – which manifests itself in many ways, as we shall consider later in this book – but of actually dwelling in the land of the shadow of death, which is part of our mortality. So what does the Light of the World prophesied by Isaiah do? He gives the "light of life," that incredible illumination which reaches into all of the dark corners of our lives and gives us thousands of candle watts to boost our energy and spiritual brightness so that we can really live. And the illumination continues through the moment of death and on to the golden streets of Heaven.

Back to the Old Testament, the Psalmist refers to the Lord as the sun, "For a day in Your courts is better than a thousand outside. I would rather stand at the threshold of the house of my God than

31

dwell in the tents of wickedness. For the Lord God is a sun and shield; The Lord gives grace and glory; No good thing does He withhold from those who walk uprightly" (Psalm 84:10). The prophet Malachi gives us another beautiful image: "But for you who fear My name, the sun of righteousness will rise with healing in its wings; and you will go forth and skip about like calves from the stall" (Mal. 4:2). As cattle ranchers, my husband and I celebrate every spring watching calves skip about, frolicking in the sunshine, rejoicing with so many newborns in the light of spring. That experience makes the comment from Malachi quite a contrast. We can get teary eyed over the idea of the "sun of righteousness" having healing in its wings, but we have to chuckle over ourselves gamboling about like calves, especially in our senior years!

All of us are in need of some kind of healing – physical, mental and/or spiritual. What an awe-inspiring image to see those healing wings of the "sun of righteousness," our Lord and Savior, enfolding us in the brightness of His healing embrace! What if we woke every morning to the new sunrise and saw that image before us? We know from psychology that imaging is a powerful tool, and the Christ of the healing wings can be the image which puts our feet on the right path for the day.

The apostle John, who catapults our faith into the fiery futuristic images of Revelation, starts his earlier gospel by referring to Jesus first as the Word and then in the Word was Life, and the Life was the Light, and the Light shone into the darkness before the Incarnation,

What are we told to do? "Walk in the light as He is in the light" (1 John: 1:7). "Shedding light" on problems is an old term we accept as meaning the gaining of understanding and wisdom to solve our problems and dark deviations from our journeys. Jesus sheds so much light that each footstep can be taken with confidence. It doesn't matter whether we are taking twelve steps to attempt recovery from addiction or whether we are taking one step in physical therapy to regain the ability to walk or whether we are simply wandering in grief or despair, Jesus' Light can make those steps clear – not necessarily easy, but clear.

Here are some more beautiful scripture references to light, first in relation to Jesus and then in relation to our own lives:

"Let us know, let us pursue knowledge of the LORD; his coming is as certain as the dawn."
HOSEA 6:3.

"In him was life, and that life was the light of all mankind."
JOHN 1:4.

"While I am in the world, I am the light of the world."
JOHN 9:5.

"Believe in the light while you have the light, so that you may become children of light."
JOHN 12:36.

"I have come into the world as a light, so that no one who believes in me should stay in darkness."
JOHN 12:46.

CHAPTER 10

The Light of the World

Coping with Darkness

E ven as we realize that Jesus is not only "the Way, the Truth, and the Life" but also illuminates the Way, we need to prayerfully consider what that Way entailed. Whether your church includes Lent in its calendar year or not, all of us recognize the need for a time to contemplate Jesus' journey to the cross and the times He spent fasting, meditating and considering His Father's will. He was the target not only of Satan but of men influenced by Satan to hamper His ministry and plot to take His life. He could not simply appear as the Light, draw everyone to Himself, and enter the kingdom of Heaven. Instead, He is our example of embracing the Light while dwelling in darkness and eventually dealing with the great darkness of death.

One March during Lent, I reveled over hiking in the desert of northern Arizona with my cousins, searching for Indian basket weavers' petroglyphs and pictographs while meditating on Jesus' walk. A poem came to me, a mixture of that ancient archaeological area and my awareness of Jesus' time in the desert.

Lenten Desert Reveries

One step after another, we travel this old river gulch where
the basket people dwelled and grew their corn,
stored it in ancient granaries in the sandstone cliffs,
and left their symbols carved and painted there, where
the ancient hunters forever track the bighorn sheep and
the spirit gods live on the walls and in the winds.
High above the golden and crimson sandstone edifices, a trio of birds
trills a lilting melody into the stillness,
while a golden marmot and long-tailed grey squirrels search
for crunchy seeds, berries, and pinyon nuts.
At the end of the canyon, cliffs reach toward the burning sun;
but from a tiny fissure, water falls into the parched air, then
meanders down, caressing moss and tiny plants, dripping softly
into pools reflecting stones and sky.

One step after another, Jesus wanders the desert paths where
ancient shepherds have guided their flocks,
searching for forage in a sun-radiating, barren land.
Among the multi-colored rocks and sifting sands, Satan
offers worldly power, stones into bread, and great renown –
rejected by just a retreating back and reverberating words.
High in the cliffs, a dove awaits John's baptizing hands, when
Jesus' feet will leave the desert paths, find the fishermen, and
walk another way that leads to Gethsemane and Golgotha.
A tiny break in the world's hard-baked crust, in human hearts, and
the springs in the desert begin to nourish birth and life,
creating pools in our world reflecting the will of God until
a bloody cross lowers, a barrier stone is rolled away, and
a flowered world welcomes all
under a now benevolent sun.

–C.J. HESER, MARCH 17, 2015

After the time of meditation and temptation, Jesus began His ministry walking at the speed of Light, literally enlightening people from the blind and lame to the spiritually blind. As we know, walking at the speed of Light did not mean just walking in glory into Paradise but instead walking to Jerusalem for the darkest night of all history, the darkness of the tomb and the black night of descent into Hell.

What do we learn from the Master as we study His years of being the Light of the World in the midst of the darkness of the world? Patience comes immediately to mind, that quality which enables people to focus on their work and have faith in the outcome. Whether Jesus was using techniques of logic to argue with the scholarly Sadducees or telling parables of shepherds and farmers to enlighten the common people, He pursued His ministry with dedication and patience, knowing that the darkness cannot prevail against the Light.

"Come unto me, all you who labor and are heavily laden, and I will give you rest. Take my yoke upon you and learn of me, for I am meek and lowly of heart, and you will find rest unto your soul" (Matt. 11:28-29). In this day, not many people are aware of what a yoke is. It is a wooden apparatus which fits over the necks of two oxen or two draft horses so that they can pull together. If we take Jesus' yoke upon us, what happens? We walk in pace with Him, and He helps us carry our burdens. What an incredible blessing! How can we blindly pass up this possibility while He stands offering a helping hand?

CHAPTER 11

The Slow Speed of Light

The speed of light, as I mentioned before, is 671 million miles per hour, a measurement always used as the fastest known process. But what about the speed of Light? Are we meant to extend the speed-obsessed pace of modern life to our spiritual lives? Do we need to stock up on mental energy drinks as we read the scriptures, so that we can race toward the Light? If we are to walk with the Light of the World, we need to take a look at the way that Jesus traveled.

To begin the study of Jesus' footsteps, I want to share another story related to Josh. When he was very young, we were struggling financially and I went back to work as a legal secretary. That meant that part of the time, Josh and his sister Anne were with a babysitter in her home. She was a wonderful, caring woman whom Anne loved, but from day one Josh was unhappy. The babysitter would get him on her lap and read to him. He would tolerate the time but not respond, and then he would return to his chosen corner with his one chosen toy for the day. The only interaction he had with other children was with his sister, who was older and had her own friends, and with any child who dared to want the toy he had – and then the interaction was anger and possessiveness. Then the day came when he didn't even want to respond to me when I came to pick the kids up after work. I could literally see him withdrawing into himself, headed for something like autism.

One day I left work early with a whole list of "have to's," and while I was contemplating my list in my head, I pulled over and found myself parked by our church, a lovely old building with beautiful stained glass windows. I decided that God wanted "pray for your son" added to the "have to's," so I went inside and knelt in front of a gorgeous depiction of the Nativity. The sun that afternoon was shining directly through Mary, and I began thinking about her role as the mother of Jesus, one we often see as long-suffering, headed for Crucifixion day. However, my thoughts went to the privileges she had been granted as the "handmaiden of the Lord." She had been there when the Son of God took His first steps, spoke His first words, ran and played, learned everything from language to numbers to carpentry work. My prayer became pleading with God to grant me the privilege of raising my little boy, giving him the stability and security he so obviously needed.

My prayer was answered, but not in the way I had expected. I came home one day to find my husband in despair, his head in his hands, and he told me that we had to sell or lose our little ranch. My despair tangled up into fury at God – how could He allow us to lose what we had worked so hard for? No home? What kind of an answer was that to my prayer?

A week later, the cattle buyer who had been hiring Doug to haul hay called and asked Doug to be the foreman for his ranch near Judith Gap. We would move in the middle of winter to a ranch too far from town for me to work. Suddenly, we found ourselves all at home, with our oldest son attending kindergarten in Judith Gap. Josh was my shadow for a couple weeks, obviously convincing himself that I would not be leaving, and then he absolutely bloomed. Impervious to cold, he went feeding with his dad a lot of days, played in the snow with his siblings, and helped me with everything he could at two years of age.

Besides being a story of answered prayer -- a lesson in how we have to trust God to answer our prayers in the best way for us – this is a story which includes a new look at Mary, smiling as Jesus took His first steps. I have always wished I could have been there, but at this point the focus needs to be on the steps themselves. If you read all of the New Testament, you will find that those steps almost always moved slowly. The pace of the speed of the Light of the World is slow. Why was Jesus moving slowly? The answer lies in the knowledge that every move He made was for the benefit of people.

CHAPTER 12

Learning to Walk at Jesus' Pace

Sunlight filters through olive branches, sending beams dappled with shadows across the ancient road. Sandled feet scatter light and shadow, dust and small stones. Bethany is but a short distance, yet the feet are tired, needing time for rest in a familiar home. Ahead are friend Lazarus, sister Martha who will feed Him well, sister Mary who will seek the Light. Here a bird pecks at seeds in grasses along the roadway, sheep baa softly in the hillside meadows, and His spirit lifts. This is His Father's world, feasting on light, finding in its beams the strength to grow and flourish. Dreaming, praying, contemplating, He finds His own strength to continue walking and to summon the Light which will illuminate mankind.

Jesus stops as He enters a town to speak to Zacchaeus in the tree, initiating a dinner invitation. In Sumaria, He visits with the woman at the well and offers her the living water. Answering the questions and needs of His disciples, healing the blind man, attending a wedding – whatever He is doing is done slowly, attentively to the needs of those around Him. Can't you picture the itinerant preacher, out there in the hills with a huge crowd of people, taking the time to feed them with the loaves and fishes before He gives the most powerful sermon of His life?

We are living in the most driven, speed-focused era people have ever experienced. Everything -- from traffic to work schedules to internet use to travel to motion picture special effects – is fast-paced. When I was a library director, people in our library complained bitterly if it took more than a minute to get an e-mail message. Only a few years before, the same people had to wait at least a couple days for something paper to arrive in the mail – and now they couldn't wait a couple minutes?

I mentioned motion picture special effects. Some years ago, I took grandchildren to see *The Tigger Movie* because I had been sharing the wonderful Winnie-the-Pooh stories of A.A. Milne with them. I found myself staring as all of the Milne characters were screaming and clinging to a tree in the middle of an avalanche as nature erupted all around. In shock, I thought of the gentle, beautiful Pooh stories, where a day might be spent looking for a pot of honey or visiting Owl for wisdom or searching for Eeyore's tail. What happened to those wonderful stories when they were adapted to the speed-demon thinking of the motion picture industry? When teachers complain about children's lack of attention span, can we answer that we have traded Pooh's sweet song for an avalanche?

If we were to interview masses of people and ask them what they needed most, often the answer would be "Time." What would the Lord of Light say? His Father has given us all the time we need, and everything beyond that is our choice. He was living in a different age -- definitely could not take an X-treme cycle buzzing through the Holy Land – but we of the age of speed desperately need to listen to Him and to slow our pace to His. No one needs to add to stress by always trying to keep up with modern day tempos, always searching for time. If we reach out and put our hand in His, we will start walking with a man who had time for what was important. If we quit our Martha bustling and sit at His feet with Mary, we will learn what is important.

When my beloved Poppo was in his 90's, he lived in an assisted living facility in my town. Every day after work, I would stop in and visit with him, watching his face light up as I came into the room. Sometimes I would play the piano for him, but mostly I would just visit, share some poems from his favorite book, and listen as he told me stories, some true, some distorted by dementia. Often when I left, he would thank me for the visit. I would always respond that the times with him were as valuable and nurturing for me as for him. At those times, in the company of my father of strong faith, I would be walking with Jesus, taking time for the most vital things in life, walking at the speed of Light. When Poppo died, I planted a tree in his memory, and every time I look at that tree, I am reminded to slow my pace, take time for others, and bask in the Light.

✦ *PART III* ✦

DARKNESS THAT LONGS FOR LIGHT

CHAPTER 13

Are there Trials and Temptations?:

From the Desert to Gethsemane

This chapter gets its title from the wonderful old hymn "What a Friend We Have in Jesus," in a verse beginning, "Are there trials and temptations? Is there trouble anywhere?" As every person reading this book knows, every one of us wrestles with trials, temptations and trouble. My excruciating experience losing Josh is personal, but it is in no way unique. Organizations full of people mourn children dead of accidents, disease and suicide and share the parents' pain of "no parents should bury their children," and so many others mourn siblings, parents, other relatives and friends. Any time I pity myself for my loss, I consider the grandsons of our cousin, who lost their toddler sister to meningitis from West Nile disease, their estranged mother to a four-wheeler accident, and their brother – twin to one of the boys – to cancer at age 17 after a long struggle. These two teenagers are mired in three major immediate family losses, tragedies beyond belief, and the arms of Jesus holding them and guiding their father and grandparents have to be their refuge and strength.

In our struggles with trials and temptations, we are not separated from Jesus, no matter how separated we may feel. Those trials and temptations actually unite us with Him, set us on the path to walk at the speed of Light. Consider Thursday of Holy Week – Holy Thursday or Maundy Thursday to many – one pivotal day which includes so many crucial facets of the jewel of our Christian faith. On that day Jesus washes the disciples' feet, instituting servitude as a holy act; offers the first Holy Communion at the Lords' Supper; identifies his betrayer; prays the most meaningful prayer of all in Gethsemane, and ultimately is betrayed and begins the horrible night before carrying His cross to Golgotha.

~~~~~~

Gethsemane

"Not my will, but Yours," He prays,
The words stifling too-human moans,
Hands clenched as drops of bloody sweat
Run rivulets down the ancient stones.

"My Father, not this cup," He pleads –
Not a crude cross on Golgotha's hill –
But His cries blend into evening's dusk
While nature and God's voice are still.

Three long years of giving and healing,
Blessing their children, touching their lives;
But eyes opened, they still see nothing,
And only the blinding sin survives.

He leans His cheek upon the cool rock
And His tears mingle with bloody fate,
While below awaits a kiss that unsheathes
The piercing sword of relentless hate.

Fear and pain would hold Him here,
Hidden in the garden's solitude still;
But Love carries Him down the path
To a waiting world and His Father's will.

–C.J. HESER, MARCH 2002

~~~~~~

What is your particular agony to bring to the garden? Do you suffer from a loss too large to bear? Do you ache over failures, over material loss, over destroyed relationships? Do you writhe in pain, confronting physical injury or disease? Do you cringe in the face of death imminent for you or for someone dear? Are any of these agonies greater than our Savior's facing crucifixion as an innocent man, knowing He will not only be deserted by His followers but by His Father and that Hell awaits Him?

When you can't bear or conquer your personal agony, it is time to join the Psalmist David when he says, "Answer me when I call, my saving God. When troubles hem me in, set me free" (Psalm 4:2). It is time to recognize the need and call upon God. It is time to surrender everything to a walk with Jesus at the speed of Light, a walk which one step at a time can lead you to a destiny in God's hands, either here or in Heaven.

Do you think that Jesus would have concluded His prayer in Gethsemane and proceeded down the path if He had believed that His story would end with the Crucifixion? Resurrection Sunday (Easter), the morning of the Resurrection of Light, is the crucial end of the story. Therefore, the question looms before us all: Can you continue with the agony and not embrace the solution? Does your faith end with the Crucifixion? Sadly, one temptation Satan puts before us is to mire in the trials and tribulations, to stay at the foot of the Cross. If we take even tentative steps to walk with our Savior, Satan will be behind us just as Jesus commanded him and our path will lead away from Golgotha to the Resurrection and the Light of eternal life.

CHAPTER 14

Walking in Darkness:
Learning to Seek the Light

All of us at some time in our lives can identify with the Israelites whom Isaiah referred to as "the people who walk in darkness." The darkness of bad sadness, worse despair, or worst depression can be consuming. In fact, the reality is that in great depression, it does not matter if there is light or not – a person cannot see it.

The sources of darkness in our lives can vary, of course. A rollicking Irish friend named Roseanne was one of the dearest parts of much of my life, beginning in the 1960's when we counseled in Girl Scout camps. From hiking to singing to teaching to stargazing together, we shared a seamless relationship. Her influence included profoundly increasing my belief in God and Jesus and my devotion to prayer and acts of faith. Roseanne was an award-winning junior high teacher who started many programs and helpful course units for kids, plus her after-school photography clubs, writing clubs and book clubs. Kids at an age when many people would cringe at the idea of teaching them were enchanted with Roseanne, and the success of her teaching was obvious in all of their lives, no matter how challenging. She loved them, taught them, reached through their barriers and pulled them into her orbit of high standards, dynamic love of English and personal dedication.

After years of successful teaching, my friend encountered a principal who opposed her free-wheeling methods and began making her life as miserable as he could. After a couple of years under his uncomfortable reign, she was diagnosed with cancer and ended up very ill with both the disease and the treatment. She taught her classes whenever she was able and orchestrated lessons for substitutes whenever she was not. Meanwhile, the principal "reorganized" the English department and eliminated her job. Too ill to go hunting for another position, she gave up. He literally destroyed her life as she perceived it, and she could not recover.

Despite slightly improving health, she spiraled into darkness with her "reason for being" gone. I say spiraled because on every turn glimmers of light reached her, times when she enjoyed life through volunteering to help needy families or through time with friends like me when we frolicked like we always had. However, one winter alcohol increased the darkness, and her spiral became a slide. Her health and ability to cope deteriorated quickly.

Beside the hospital bed in her living room, I played old favorites on the piano and recalled precious memories when we had hiked together in the Beartooth Mountains, counseled Girl Scout camp sessions together, spent Christmas with her Irish grandparents and family and so on. My friend had always embraced the deepest Christian faith I have ever seen, and I referred to that over and over as I witnessed her fading away. Then she talked to me, and obviously Jesus' Light had again touched her life. When her time came to die, I know that she not only saw that bright light described by those who have near-death experiences; she also grasped the hand that was offered to help her again walk with the Light.

One thing Jesus wanted His Disciples and followers to learn was that appreciation of the Light comes as people understand and wish to escape the darkness. The "good news" of the Bible is full of Light, true enlightenment, and it is available to anyone willing to read or listen. Just as depression can block the Light, it can also block the Word. We need to help each other get beyond that point, to offer a "hand up" towards walking in the Light together. A vital lesson learned in the process is that every time we offer help, we re-establish our own journey.

You see, the difference between walking IN darkness and walking WITH Jesus is the preposition; WITH gives us a companion on the journey. Those suffering from depression, from any condition which leaves them in the darkness, learn that it is a solitary, lonely journey. Groping in the darkness saps the spirit, tires the body, and addles the mind. Help lies in reaching out and grasping the hand which Jesus offers. Then the Light dawns. Isaiah continues, "They that dwell in the land of the shadow of death, upon them hath the light shined" (Isa. 9:2). In addition, we can find that the journey is no longer solitary because others are grasping His hand as well. We can reach for the people who personify the Light – those "saints" all around us whom the Light shines through.

CHAPTER 15

Energy from the Son:
Combating Grief and Depression

I f you have ever experienced deep grief and/or depression, you know that one horrible, pervasive symptom is a loss of energy. When my son's death was the overwhelming factor in my life, I found myself wanting to stay in bed, pull the covers up over my head, and black out the world. I who am never listless was devastatingly so. I who had always embraced life with enthusiasm was shunning both the positive and the possibilities. I who had geared my life to strong productivity was lethargic and ineffective.

Isn't it ironic that at a time when we seem to be unable to sleep, we actually can sleep our lives away? That at a time when we are immersed in blackness, our instinct is to shut out any light that there is? That at a time when we need healing the most, we are the most certain that healing is impossible? That at a time when we need Jesus most, we allow ourselves to be cynical about His ability to be a force in our lives? People who experience tragedy often move from asking God "Why?" to cursing God "Because."

My grandmother talked about women at the turn of the 20th century who still believed in wearing "widow's weeds," somber black apparel worn every day for the proper year of mourning. Black was draped on houses, hung on doors, constantly displayed as a kind of respect for the dead, and black is still a part of funerals. The reason I bring up the use of black for mourning is that it seems to have its origin in the idea of an outward expression of an inward feeling. To have any light and color in lives dealing with death seemed at worst disrespectful and at least frivolous.

Of course, mourning is connected with death; but I contend that depression – in whatever form, including clinical depression -- is a kind of mourning as well. When we are depressed, something has at least temporarily died inside of us. Sometimes it is hormonal or genetic, stress- or trauma-related, but no matter what the causes, some energy source dies. No wonder it seems impossible to open our eyes, let alone move on with our lives. Those who move from being depressed to being suicidal often cite the lack of energy as one of the compelling reasons not to keep trying to make life work.

We think of Jesus in terms of His teachings and His healing, but if we examine His life more carefully, we can see His boundless energy. He is the man who commanded storms to become calm, the man who walked incredible distances to speak to crowds, perform miracles, and give of Himself endlessly with little sleep. He walked and fasted in the desert and then accomplished His ministry in three short years. Think about any three years of your life, when you felt productive, and then compare what you did to what Jesus did. What was His source of energy? He is the Word, existing in union with the Father from the beginning of time, manifesting the Holy Spirit, and of course His energy comes from His very existence.

When suffering from depression, we often draw the curtains, physically and metaphorically, to shut out the light while we muddle in the darkness. Do we not do the same thing to Jesus, letting our obsessions with ourselves and our grief obscure the Light of the World? What happens when we open that curtain, look our Lord in the face, and let our craving for Light take over? If we begin to walk with Him, pray to Him, study His word, and focus on His healing instead of our suffering, we can find the darkness of our depression fading. Notice that I said fading, not immediately disappearing.

Do grief or other sources of depression go away? I can attest to the fact that they continue to circle around, to crop up in unforeseen places and moments. However, walking with the Light of the World can become a daily habit, beginning with talking to Him in the morning when you rise and continuing to the point when you talk to Him as you fall asleep. If you reach that place, then you will find that grief and depression can be met head on and relegated to their proper place in your life. Not gone, but handled; not gone, but given to the Redeemer whose Love and Light never fails; not gone, but so submerged in Light that they cannot exert dark power over our lives and loves.

CHAPTER 16

Blindness:

Perceiving God's Goodness in a Dark World

O ther than at Gethsemane and Golgotha, nowhere else in the New Testament do we have a stronger picture of Jesus than in His healing of the blind man. The story is so simple at first, with Jesus putting mud on the eyes of a man blind from birth and telling him just to go wash the mud off in a pool. The man receives his sight, and others including his parents are impressed. However, the story gets more complicated when the Pharisees have a problem with performing healing on the Sabbath and with Jesus doing things which show His godliness. Although questioned and accused, the blind man holds firm to His conviction that he received sight miraculously.

Sight is a sense which so many of us take for granted even when we depend upon it so heavily. Anyone confronted with glaucoma or macular degeneration begins to look at that sense very differently, and of course those who never have sight or lose it tragically certainly understand what a major force it is. However, this Bible story deals with much more than one sense. When the blind man comes back to Jesus, he finds that he has seen the Son of God. His eyes are opened in a much more profound way than just to see the world around him. And the Pharisees are accused of being mired in their own "blindness."

The Light of the World is infinitely more precious and important to us as He sheds His light on our total lives rather than just our eyes. In Victorian stories about the "Survivors Club," a group who survived war but gathered to deal with the damage to their bodies and minds, the talented novelist Mary Balogh has a character make this observation about a blind man in *Only Beloved*: "He has learned to give light to the darkness in which he must live out his life, and in so doing he has shed light upon those of us who think we can see." Here again we have the enigma that dealing with blindness can give insight which is more powerful than a physical sense.

All of us struggle with darkness at some time in our lives, and some of us struggle with it far more than others. Addictions form the darkness against which a dear friend of mine must do battle, but she has learned to seek help before she succumbs these days. Her Christian faith and her own will to overcome the forces which threaten to blind her again have given her the power of the Light. Like Mary Balogh's blind man, she "sheds light" on her family and friends so that we see more clearly the Light of the World as well.

What is your blindness? What is it that shuts you away from God's love? Is it grief which embitters you against God, thinking that He has turned His back on you when instead He continues His love while you turn your back on Him? Is it a craving, either for something like alcohol, drugs, or gambling or instead for worldly riches, success or power when all of these can cloak us in blackness? Is it your own selfish needs and wants, so obscuring your perception that, like Narcissus of myth, you can see only yourself reflected in your obsessive pool?

The cure for such blindness is not just in opening our eyes. It lies in opening our entire beings to the Light. Jesus knows that we will not suddenly be cured of blindness, and so He offers His gentle guidance to help us in our darkness. Just as our eyes can "get used to the dark," we can lean on Jesus until we can see enough at least to find our daily way. The lesson we have to learn, however, is that when we begin to find our way, we need His presence even more. Then we get the promise that nothing can separate us from the love of God, and that includes our own blindness and sinfulness. Think about the beloved hymn "Amazing Grace": "I once was lost but now am found, was blind but now I see." It was written by a slave trader who despaired over what he had done to other human beings and whose influence led to the abolition of slavery in England. The hymn obviously strikes a chord with many who know that at least at some point all of us are lost and blind and need to trust the Light of the World to bring us to the point at which we are found and are able to see.

CHAPTER 17

Eclipse:

When Jesus' Light Is Hidden

In September of 2015, people all over the world watched in awe the spectacle of a total lunar eclipse, this one made special by being the eclipse of a "blue moon," the second full moon in a month, as well as a "blood moon" with red overtones. The pictures are amazing. Many of us can also remember solar eclipses, partial or full, and that gripping feeling of fascination with having the sun blocked temporarily. The essential ingredient, of course, is that word "temporarily," and undoubtedly people have had to reassure children that the sun is still there and will be shining again soon. I never think of eclipses without thinking of Mark Twain's *A Connecticut Yankee in King Arthur's Court*, where the "Yankee" saves his own life by pretending to "put out" the sun because he knows when an eclipse is occurring. The ignorant people are certain he has the power to extinguish the sun permanently unless he gets all demands met.

In the chapter pertaining to depression, I mentioned that when people are in deep depression, they cannot see the light even if it is there. This is an eclipse situation. You and I know that despite the darkness of an eclipse, the sun or moon is still there and will be back in our view of things soon. However, those in depression can lose that knowledge, either forget or deny that the Light of God previously in their lives is still there. If you or someone you care about gets to that point, help is strongly needed. Medication and other treatments are available and sometimes very necessary, and a doctor or psychologist can deal with that part of depression prevention. However, medication is not enough. Beyond medical and institutional help, a Christian counselor, minister, or friend knowledgeable of the true nature of depression can offer assistance in a return to the Light. As soon as Light starts to reappear, reinforcement from those people plus Bible study and uplifting activities can intensify the end of the eclipse.

We Christians need to remember that prevention measures are needed to defend against future depression. Too often we go to God in prayer only when we are in trouble and focus on the Light only when our world is dark. Instead, we need to weather the eclipses, which are going to happen to everyone at some time, by having established our walk with the Light of the World as a daily, permanent action. Like every other condition which I have mentioned in this book, depression begs for the healing of Jesus, the Light of His presence and love, and the understanding that joy cannot truly be ours until we fully embrace His love and grace.

A good friend of ours found himself at the "bottom of the bottle," having lost his marriage, his relationship with his children, and his reasons for living because of his alcoholism. Talk about an eclipse situation! Fortunately for him and for many others, he crawled toward the Light through his Christian faith and Alcoholics Anonymous. He became a leader in that organization, celebrating his years of not drinking by giving others a strong "leg up" toward the answers he had found. He was one of the ones who grasped the Lord's hand and then reached out for others' hands to help them begin and continue their walks at the speed of Light as well. That hand never let go when someone slipped, and that faith never waivered no matter what he confronted.

He was a man who personified the Light, and his self-assigned work for others continued through the days that he was dying of a heart condition and still found the words to guide the young man in the hospital bed next to him toward AA meetings to change his life. The greatest manifestation of his faith in Jesus was to seek the Light not only for himself but for others as well, and I knew as we bid him farewell at his memorial service that Jesus was saying, "Well done, thou good and faithful servant."

The major lesson from Alcoholics Anonymous is manifested in the leadership of our friend who understood so strongly the need for the consistent walk which must be one day at a time, renewed with each dawn and picked up again every time we stumble. Often the source of an eclipse in our lives, like a natural eclipse, is something beyond our control. However, we also need to be aware of those things which we can control – and that brings us to the next part of our reflections.

✦ *PART IV* ✦

DARKNESS WE CHOOSE

CHAPTER 18

Walking Out of Step:

Human Choices and Jesus' Path

ave you ever watched – or been – the novice member of the high school marching band, struggling to do everything right, sometimes confusing left and right feet, sometimes concentrating so hard on getting it right that the result is lagging behind and then trying to catch up? I'm sure the same thing happens to green Army recruits, although the repercussions are probably more severe. The point, of course, is that walking in step is not always accomplished easily because we put in some effort or have good intentions. If walking with Jesus were easy, then the Disciples would have had it made as soon as they signed on to be Fishers of Men. Instead, we read in the New Testament how they all struggle and stumble, some fatally like Judas, all in various levels of lack of understanding and at times lack of faith.

Simon Peter, one of the most amazing men in all history – the rock on which Jesus established His church – found himself walking out of step far too often, sometimes clearly in the wrong direction and most often because he was trying to walk ahead of Jesus. Peter's strengths turned to weaknesses any time he tried to take things into his own hands instead of really listening to Jesus. Examples are when, right after witnessing the miracle of Jesus feeding the multitude, he asks to join Jesus in walking on the water and falters because of doubt and fear; also, at the Last Supper, he refuses to let Jesus wash his feet, then when Jesus insists he wants both his hands and feet washed and again Jesus has to remind him that only His original offer stands. After Jesus renames Simon as Peter and calls him the rock upon which He will build the church, within a short time Peter argues with Jesus about His prediction of His death and Resurrection.

Can you imagine how Peter felt the night when he heard the cock crow after denying Jesus three times? When Jesus warned him, Peter pooh-poohed the very idea, sure that he had the answers. After all, wasn't he the one who had identified Jesus as the Son of God? But just a few hours later, Peter's steps plunged him into a darkness as chilly as a lake in the Rockies right after the spring thaw. Notice that the next time we read about Peter, he is stepping into the empty tomb, realizing that the Light of the World has conquered all darkness including the depths of Hell.

Why was Peter – this intelligent, strong man -- out of step? When the cock crows, we have our answer. The first factor was fear, understandable in a time of persecution of anyone connected with Jesus. However, fear is still a major motivator in our lives. Instead of stepping boldly, embracing the invitation of Jesus to walk in the Light, people creep in the darkness of addiction, abuse, crime, and so much more because of fear. Fear caused Peter to get out of step, to forget all that Jesus had told him and the other followers about His coming death and Resurrection, to drop his eyes to his staggering feet and lose sight of the future which Jesus had prepared him for. Second, in addition to walking in fear, Peter was not only denying Jesus – he was practicing denial. Denial works for a little while, long enough for Peter to back away from his questioners, long enough for us to convince ourselves that we don't need the Light or can even generate it for ourselves. However, as any counselor can tell you, denial not only does not work for the long haul, it actually generates its own trap, its own darkness.

What we need to comprehend is that even when Peter was denying Him, Jesus was in charge. He had claimed Peter for His own, needed Him for the work of the Kingdom, and understood Peter's need to learn the lesson of the futility of succumbing to fear and denial. How could Peter lead the fledgling church through the challenges and horrors of the time ahead if he was not in step with Jesus, overcoming the impediments which had tripped him during the time before Jesus' death? The Peter we meet in the times after Jesus' Resurrection is a man who has overcome fear and denial to the point of being able to establish the early church and to eventually return to Rome to his own horrible death on a cross. As he walked toward the end of his life, he was 100 percent in step with his Savior.

CHAPTER 19

Out of Step:

When Doubt Steps In

As we reflect on the problems of being out of step, let us turn to another Disciple, a man barely mentioned in the stories of the New Testament until after Jesus' death – the man known to most of us as Doubting Thomas. The Disciples, who with the exception of Thomas have already seen the risen Christ, are gathered in a room when Jesus appears to them. Knowing of the Resurrection, they recognize Jesus at once and accept Him as their Lord – all except Thomas. You see, Thomas, like Peter and like all of the Disciples at times, was out of step with Jesus; although, where Peter was getting into trouble walking ahead, Thomas was lagging behind, seeking the Light but not yet able to be in step.

Thomas was not sinning in asking to see and touch Jesus' wounds; instead he was confirming his faith. For this moment, he was just following behind, and for that reason Jesus does not chastise him. In the act of seeing and touching Jesus' wounds, of course, Thomas gets up to speed and can now function as a Disciple of the future. Imagine how the church could benefit from Thomas and his experience! Those with doubts would have someone who understands, one who has been through the difficulty of doubt and now believes with all his heart. I'll bet that when you are thinking of the "gifts" which God uses from among His people, you haven't included the gift of faith in the midst of doubt. Put it on the list!

Rejecting God, turning one's back to Him, is a sin, but doubting is not. In fact, I believe that in most cases, people who have never doubted need to examine the depth of their faith. Doubt means that we are truly looking for answers, for understanding, for illumination as strong as the Light of His presence. Look once again at Jesus' reaction to "Doubting Thomas." He did not rebuke this man who wanted to see and touch – to have empirical proof – before he was certain of Jesus' return from the grave. Granted, He praised those who believe without seeing; but He accepted Thomas' requests without judgment; I get the impression that He was just glad that Thomas wanted to have his doubts answered and then believe with the rest. Many proclaimers of the Good News suffered, sinned, doubted and struggled before they reached the point where they were so certain of the Lord and their walks with Him that they could proclaim it to all. A couple of books I highly recommend in this area are *Confessions* by Saint Augustine and *The Seven Storey Mountain* by Thomas Merton. These are not easy reads, but if you read at least parts of them you will discover amazing stories of changing from out of step to in step with our Lord.

Do you suppose that God shook His head sometimes over Moses, Abraham, Jeremiah, Peter, Paul, and the other significant leaders in the Bible? You know He shook His head over Adam and Eve, watching them walk out of the Garden of Eden in their new clothes, giving up Paradise because of their sinful ways. Would we have done differently? Before we get too cocky over what we would have done better, we need to take a look at our lives so far and weigh whether we would be basking under the trees in the garden or out wielding a hoe in barren soil along with Adam. The point, though, is that God was with all of these people, and when it was clear that His people would never be able to overcome their own sinfulness, He sent His Son to overcome the darkness with Light.

So what do we do when we are out of step? First, we need to recognize and acknowledge the fact that we are trying to surge ahead without Jesus' direction or we are lagging behind because we are forgetting or ignoring the need to walk with Him. Second, we need to go back to the scriptures or an inspiring Christian book for inspiration, pray for help, and readjust our journeys. One of my favorite sources for such readjustment, other than the Bible, is Norman Vincent Peale's *The Power of Positive Thinking* because that wonderful minister provides such inspiring wisdom for anyone needing a boost in walking in step with the Lord. He is an example of people who have found the way to walk right with the Light of the World and to share that Light with readers far into the future.

CHAPTER 20

Losing the Spotlight:

Breaks in the Rhythm

Have you ever been at a play when the person in charge of lighting fails to keep the spotlight on the actor or singer? It can be almost comical, or at times embarrassing, as the spotlight moves around trying to settle on the right person or to follow that person accurately. One can sing, dance, or deliver lines without a spotlight, but the audience becomes distracted by the maneuverings of the light and fails to follow the performer well.

In our daily walk, whether we are working, caring for family, playing, or following other pursuits, we need God's Light with us. Unlike the spotlight operator at the play, God offers His Light steadily through His Son. If we find ourselves in the shadows, it is we who have miscued or lost the rhythm of the dance. Unlike the patterns of walking too fast or too slow, these times out of the Light are momentary or sporadic. A loss of focus, an instant of forgetting our purpose, a poor choice of direction – all of these things can take us away from the Light long enough to affect not only our lives but the lives of those in our personal audience.

Although all of us have times of grief, sadness, or depression when the Light is far away, most of us have far more times when we simply make mistakes, make poor choices, forget to say the right thing or slip and say the wrong thing, succumb to temptation, hurt or neglect someone and falter in our roles and relationships. We temporarily stumble in our travels with our Lord of Light. If we study the scriptures closely, we see people bungle and lose the Light on a regular basis. Most of them don't make irreparable mistakes like Lot's wife, who ended up a pillar of salt, or Adam and Eve, who had to leave the garden. Instead, they break a commandment like David's adultery, they hesitate in their mission like Moses, they choose the wrong companion like Samson, they flee from responsibility like Jonah, or they make poor life choices like Jesus' friend Martha.

The point is that the spotlight is still there. We can resume our rightful roles, rediscover our purpose, and continue our walk in the Light. Three things are required: our recognition of our errors, our true repentance and our effort to atone and do better. Straying from the Light and then returning with renewed dedication can make us stronger and more focused. I mentioned David, who strayed in a major way. He expressed his great sorrow and repentance in his Psalms, and from that point on he became the great king God needed. David in the spotlight was not only an exemplary follower of God but also the ancestor of Jesus. God loved him and used him just as he was.

What do we need to learn from David? God loved us enough to send us our Redeemer, He accepts us exactly as we are, and He continues to focus His spotlight on our lives so that we can live in the Light. We need to try hard to do His will, we need to pray that He "lead us not into temptation and deliver us from evil," and we need to be conscious of our need for repentance and Light. Beyond that, we need to love ourselves. Remember that Jesus commanded us to love others as ourselves. Did you look in the mirror this morning and see someone lovable? If not, perhaps you have strayed into the shadows and lost the spotlight. Return to the mirror and look at the person reflected there as God sees you: the one He has loved before you were conceived, the one He has sent His Son for, the one He has promised eternal life with Him. Now can you love that person in the mirror? Who are we to question the worthiness of someone God loves that much?

We can glory in Jesus' love for us and love the person in the mirror, as long as the focus remains on Jesus and we accept the Christian responsibility for sharing the Light with others. We have to acknowledge that if we stumble and lose the Light, we may affect others' lives as well. Then we need to ask forgiveness not only of our God but of others we may have affected before we can resume our place in the Light and our true journey with Him. If our eyes are on our Savior and His Light, we can shine not only for ourselves but for others.

CHAPTER 21

The Light Dims:

Times of Sin, Times of Doubt

A Catholic theologian once spoke to an adult study group I was part of about the much-argued theory of Limbo, the place invented by theologians for unbaptized infants or unsanctified adults to try to explain what happens to people who do not come under Jesus' command that all must believe and be baptized to enter Heaven. The theologian's point for our class was that if we define Heaven as being with Jesus for eternity and Hell as not being with Jesus for eternity, then Limbo could not be the solution.

Theological quibbling aside, we know that times exist when we are not walking at the speed of Light, not in step with our Savior, because of sin. Sin is not just doing wrong; it actually involves choosing to turn away from the Light, to embrace thoughts or actions which hide us from Jesus. Does that mean that the Light of the World is no longer in our lives? On the contrary, these are the times when Jesus is standing at the door knocking, and we have just chosen to close the door. What is needed to open the door is repentance, which interestingly enough is translated as "to turn," in the sense of changing one's mind, and thus fits nicely with our thoughts on conversion.

Sin interrupts our walking at the speed of Light simply because no one can follow or keep in step with someone who cannot be seen. The barrier of sin is far worse than a horse with blinders, those harness parts designed to keep the horse's eyes on the "straight and narrow" and minimize spooking at scary things off to the side. Sin is literally blinding, reminding us that it is not Jesus who creates the barrier when we sin, it is us. God created us with free will, that amazing tie with enlightenment which enables us to make the choice to yoke ourselves to Him and walk in the Light. That same free will allows the Devil to delve into our choices and assist us in erecting the barrier which obscures the Light.

If sin becomes a total way of life, then the darkness can become complete and the Devil can claim us. That state is far worse than just getting out of step or temporarily allowing ourselves to be distracted. St. John uses strong words when he deals with the sin of denying the Light. In 1 John 1:6, he writes, "If we claim to have fellowship with Him and yet walk in the darkness, we lie and do not live out the truth." John's words are aimed at the "Sunday Christians," the hypocrites who love to talk about fellowship and then live everyday lives in sin and denial of the very Lord they profess.

Yet even when we sin, lie or in any way choose the darkness, the Light of the World is still there, and hope is offered as the beloved hymn "Amazing Grace" reminds us, no matter how dark we have allowed our lives to become. For most of us, sin does not become a total way of life but instead a dimming of the Light, a lack of focus as though we had the lens cover on our personal camera and were wondering why we could not view what we wanted to photograph. However, stepping foot off the "narrow path" remains serious simply because a lack of Light is always an impediment to a full life with our Lord.

God created us with free will and with minds capable of doubt, rebellion and sin. In my college days, as part of a campus ministry, I dealt strongly with doubt. A Christian from childhood, I suddenly found myself facing the cold facts that friends were dying in the Vietnam War and of drug overdoses in Haight-Ashbury and that our capitalistic society and very often our churches didn't have all the answers. I doubted, I searched, I ached, and I made some sinful choices. Then one day I took my rebellion and sin to God in profound prayer and found the Light again. The miracle was that the Light was now more intense and my walk at the speed of Light was surer and stronger.

I like to think that God said, "Let there be light" twice – once during Creation, and once when He sent our Savior. Despite our natural tendency to sin, to rebel, and to lose sight of the Light, we can turn back to God with sincere repentance and a great "Amen." Then we can embrace the Light once more.

CHAPTER 22

Closing the Shutters:
Self-Imposed Darkness

M any things that rob us of the Light are not of our own choosing. Illness, serious injury, death, bouts with sadness or depression and estrangement are all things that can come into our lives without our invitation. Other things are a result of our very human mistakes and stumbling, and again we cope and hopefully change what we can. We can make choices to shut out the Light, just as we can close shutters on a house to cover windows. At the time such choices are made, our thoughts are not on shutting out Jesus or His Light, of course. Our thoughts are on ourselves and how we can exercise that free will for our own "needs." So we need that drink or that drug or that sexual encounter or that gambling bet or anything else that can help us temporarily. Such choices for many people lead to addictions, our own "self-imposed darkness."

Nothing can cause us to stagger out of step with our Lord and ourselves or to lose sight completely of His Light worse than addictions. They not only obscure our commitments to our faith, they obscure our commitments to marriage, parenthood, jobs, financial responsibilities and other adult obligations. Addictions can expand beyond irresponsibility to crime to support the addictions.

All of these things are outward signs of being sadly out of step, and the fact that they are results of our own choices doesn't make them more or less important in God's eyes.

Let's go back to the analogy of the shutters on the house. Why do we close shutters? Very often the closing is a result of a storm coming and our need to escape. Unfortunately, for many people addictions are such escape mechanisms – escape from pain or loneliness or frustration. All of us can understand the need for escape, as we do through such things as reading and the movies. The difference lies in what we are escaping to: choices like reading, if taken to extremes, can interfere with our productivity and possibly our perception of reality but otherwise are not harmful. Escape to addictions like alcohol, drugs and gambling are, of course, a different matter. Closing the shutters that way creates a darkness which makes it incredibly difficult to re-embrace the Light.

Whether we suffer from addictions ourselves or suffer with someone else who is a victim of addictions, we need to keep one thing in mind. Despite our sins, our bad choices, and sometimes our life-altering addictions, the God who created us and His Son who saved us continue to want the best for us. Jesus continues to walk beside us, waiting for us to see the Light. Because of Jesus' all-empowering love, we have it within our power to overcome addictions, sometimes on our own but more often with help. God bestows gifts of understanding and healing on doctors and workers in addiction clinics and hospitals. We cannot achieve success, even with their help, if we lose our focus on God's role in our lives. Overcoming addictions is not just a matter of "will power." It is a matter of turning over our lives to God so that His will be done. The immense strength necessary for overcoming addictions can be ours when we grasp God's strength and set our feet on the road one day at a time by Jesus' side.

In case I seem to be oversimplifying something which is immense and complex, I want you to know that I have known a number of people with addictions. All of them agreed that the pull of addiction is too strong to be overcome without constant Light. One person who was very dear to me was a man of faith who nonetheless could allow his gaze to falter and to focus on so-called "friends" who altered his walk with Jesus. He would get addiction treatment, set his feet on the path with the Light, and then return to these people and their lifestyle including drinking. Then he would lose sight of the Light again and fall right back into the self-made darkness. Notice that despite others' influence, it was self-made darkness, because God reminds us again and again in His Word that the choice is always ours.

As for those of us who do not have to engage in this daily battle, we need to keep all those with addictions in our prayers. If they are acquaintances, we need to encourage them to get help and to persevere. Most of all, we need to put this darkness into the hands of the Savior who calms storms and heals afflictions.

CHAPTER 23

Journey to Dawn:
Combating the Darkness of Hatred

Journey to Dawn
Twisted, gnarly, and grizzled,
Discarded driftwood on the edge of
A thrashing sea, hatred tangled itself
In my stumbling footsteps.
Panicked and pain filled, I floundered,
Grasping for lifelines, then letting it
Consume my nighttime and
Obscure my daylight.
The waves dragged me outward and outward;
No ebb tide return, just further asea,
Groping, succumbing, overwhelmed
By watery, paralyzing mortality,
Until, abandoned like flotsam,
I washed up on the coastline of reality,
Gasping for enough oxygen to exist,
Enough brainwaves to forget.
Funny how pitifully trivial driftwood
Looks in the luminescence of dawn
As the sea caresses the beach and shorebirds
Coax the softer world into singing.

--C.J. HESER, FEBRUARY 2016

I wrote this poem at a time when I had prayerfully found release from a debilitating hatred in my life, something I was carrying around and being poisoned by as though I had cancer cells growing within me. Many of us have discovered that hatred does much more damage to the hater than to the hated. In fact, hatred is as futile as revenge because both of them rise from a source definitely not in step with Jesus and His Light.

Hatred is in a league with sin. If we know that God is Love, then definitely hatred is not of God despite its existence as a very human emotion. Anger -- if it comes from belief like the anger Jesus expressed toward Satan in the desert, toward the dishonest moneychangers defiling the temple, and toward the self-righteous Pharisees who were discrediting the very faith they pretended to represent – can be justified. However, if anger becomes hatred, it becomes a path which can lead us far from the Lord of Light.

Back to the poem, notice what happens in the dawn light. The driftwood now looks pitiful, just as our hatred can be viewed as sad and insignificant when we finally confront it. When God created us in His image, He made us to be like Him in love for ourselves and for others. It has to go against the grain to choose hatred and then feed and maintain it.

How can we combat hatred? We can't just turn off a mind focused on a strong emotion like hatred. However, we can dilute that hatred by opening our minds to other things. Sometimes it helps just to do something physical. I know a couple of men who can split a pile of firewood and with every blow of the axe find a release for hatred, and I know several men and women who use long-distance running for the same purpose. Some people clean their houses right down to the woodgrain in the flooring, but again make sure you aren't thinking hateful thoughts but instead are focused on the task. If you try one of these possibilities, make sure your senses are opened up, so that you hear and see every blow of the axe or every running step on the pavement or every stroke of the mop or broom.

If physical effort doesn't fit you for some reason, try something gentler, but make sure both your mind and senses are engaged. For many of us, a long walk or bike ride in nature works. See how many things you can see, hear and smell. During a walk is a wonderful time to pray because we can "tune in" to creation and let it fill us. If you are sitting quietly because you need down time or are ill or aching, study the scriptures or bring nature to yourself. I have a great day planner with luscious photos of natural phenomena accompanied by the words of the great Christian yoga philosopher Paramahansa Yogananda. I can look at a gorgeous picture of a sunset over the ocean and read, "When one contemplates the expanse of ocean and sky, he escapes momentarily the confinements of finite matter and glimpses the Infinite." I may be confined to my living room, but my mind is with the ocean and sky reflecting God's light.

Hatred not only creates darkness but depends upon it. A significant biblical example of hatred is the story of Judas, who chose to turn away from the Light to the darkness of his hatred-inspired Zealot expectations and thus destroy not only Jesus but himself. In contrast to Judas, Disciples like John learned that the more Light we seek, the more Light we gather to ourselves as we walk with Jesus, the more the darkness of hatred will have to run for the corners of our lives and hopefully disappear completely.

CHAPTER 24

The Inconstant Moon:
Light We Cannot Trust

Remember Juliet in her famous balcony scene when Romeo is swearing his love to her and makes the mistake of swearing by the moon? She tells him, "O, swear not by the moon, the inconstant moon,/ That monthly changes in her circled orb,/ Lest that thy love prove likewise variable" (*Romeo and Juliet*, Act 2, Scene 2).

In St. Paul's letters in the New Testament we are warned over and over that we will be beckoned by the "antichrist" and offered false testimony and false answers. Sometimes this beckoning obviously comes from Satan, tempting us to sin. But more often the false testimony and false answers are subtle and come from sources that we are inclined to trust.

I have referred to my very dear uncle, a talented mechanic and musician, who was a victim of alcoholism. When things got really bad, he would get help, twice by going through a complete "dry out" at a specialized institution. When he returned, he would seek out his friends, particularly those who played in a dance band with him. Unfortunately, they would encourage him to have a drink with them, and soon he would again submerge in the depths of his addiction.

Most of us would see light in friendship. But in the case of "friends" who don't really support the best in us, that light is as inconstant as the moon in its dark phase. Many people who seek light in marriage find it if that marriage is based on the principles found in Corinthians, where love is defined in so many ways as compassionate, forgiving and self-sacrificing. Many others seek light in marriage only to find that the light in the relationship is inconstant as the moon and perhaps false, elusive and destructive.

False light can be found in a number of forms. For example, meditation is strongly supported in our society for mental and spiritual health. However, if meditation is focused on our navels and on our own selfish needs, it can provide undependable light, if any. Interviews with a number of psychopathic killers have revealed dependence upon meditation as preparation for horrendous acts. At a less frightening level, meditation can lead to selfish, secular decisions which prove to be harmful in the long run.

My answer to people with interest in meditation is to suggest prayer combined with meditation. Prayer connects us to God and Jesus and promises us true and constant Light. In our meditation we may struggle with thorny questions and not easily arrive at answers, but if we are praying, we are expanding the meditation to include God's input and Jesus' guidance. Combine that with Scripture readings that reveal Jesus' words related to people's dilemmas, and the Light becomes something constant that can truly enlighten our lives.

Sadly, false or at least inconstant light can radiate from people who claim to believe yet do not truly follow Jesus. Using religion to be judgmental, vindictive, and even cruel is a sad distortion of the light, yet some so-called Christians believe that their faith justifies those kinds of thoughts and actions. Tragically, their false "light" can actually turn people away from Christianity.

The inconstant moon shows up in another way that will not sit well with people who work hard on their own strength and self-esteem. God created us to be strong and self-reliant – after all, He needs the Noahs and Joshuas and St. Pauls in the world to carry leadership roles. However, if that strength and self-reliance becomes nothing but ourselves, shutting out God, it is guaranteed to be inconstant. Because we are imperfect creatures, we will falter and fail at times. Then where does the light go? When Jesus said that we are the "light of the world," he was referring to our reflection of His Light. Our light can shine before others to show them His way only if we are reflecting Him. Step away from His Light, and we become as inconstant as the moon.

So how do we know whether the light is true or false, constant or inconstant? Take Jesus' hand, read His words, listen to His true followers, pray to Him regularly, and open your heart and life to Him. The true Light will be with you, even in your darkest days, even when you are wondering if you can trust anyone or anything. Join David in knowing that the Lord is your shepherd, and the result will be that "surely goodness and mercy shall follow me all the days of my life, and I will dwell in the house of the Lord forever" (Psa. 23:6). Can it get any better than that?

✦ *PART V* ✦

FACETS OF LIGHT

CHAPTER 25

Forest Fires and Light:

Life Experiences that Bring Growth

The forest sparkles in the sunshine after a rain, with jeweled droplets along every branch. New-growth pines just a few feet taller than I am brighten acres of Yellowstone National Park, all shades of green letting light and shadow dance across the dappled forest floor, splashed with magenta fireweed, crimson Indian paintbrush, and lavender blue Scottish harebells. Filled with sounds of creek water bubbling over stones, squirrels chattering from treetops, and Steller's jays jabbering at each other, the fresh-scented forest appeals to every sense and radiates peace.

Almost thirty years ago, I drove this same road, witnessing the ravages of forest fires so hot that they left almost no ground growth despite crowning – traveling through the tops of the trees in high winds, partly created by the fires themselves. I love this magnificent park and revel in its sylvan beauty. With tear-dimmed eyes I took in the horrible devastation, the blackened world of nature ruined so completely that even the high blue skies seemed compromised. No intelligent, caring person would welcome forest fires, which endanger lives and property while destroying plants and animal habitats.

However, where did those beautiful young trees of today come from? A study of trees like lodgepole pines reveals that the cones of these trees cannot germinate unless they are at a very high temperature created only by fire. Equally amazing, the young trees which grow from those seeds caused to germinate by forest fires actually have a fire retardant in their bark which prevents them from burning in future fires as they grow to maturity. In other words, only the old trees burn, and as a result, forest renewal is guaranteed. The result is that forest fires become a natural part of the Creator's design.

What are the forest fires in your life – those experiences which devastate and blacken your world, move you from light to darkness? Everyone has those fires, sometimes momentary and sometimes long lasting, and just like my favorite natural environments, our lives can suffer horribly. Our entire landscapes can lose all of the beauty and elements which enable us to live in peace. When we reach the point of greatest loss, we have the choice of miring into the ashes and losing ourselves in the blackness or of trusting the God who made us and loves us.

This God created the lodgepole pine literally to rise from the ashes like the phoenix, an event which cannot happen without a forest fire. The same God created us in His image and asks us to turn to Him when we experience the forest fires of our lives so that He can nourish the seeds of our new growth. How do we grow when all we can see is the burnt stumps of our past, when the sights, sounds and smells of life are obscured by darkness? What is necessary for growth after germination? The nourishment of water and soil – our daily bread – but more than that. We need the Light. If we walk with the Lord in His Light, we will grow from our experiences of darkness, moving into the future which He offers us.

Back to the question of what you want for your life. You can dwell only in the blackened forest – not a bad description of depression

– and stop your spiritual life with the Crucifixion. Can you realize what would have happened to the Disciples and other followers if their spiritual lives had ended with the Crucifixion? Do you realize that every word of the Bible after Adam and Eve's sinful choice and expulsion from the Garden of Eden was leading to Jesus' life and death, but most of all to His Resurrection? Without the Resurrection, all is darkness, and that is as true in your personal life as it is in the lives of every believer in the Bible. How can we make the choice to dwell in a spiritual life ending with the Crucifixion?

The other choice is to survive, to grow, and to walk in the Light of the Resurrection every day. What about those forest fires we cannot survive, those devastating illnesses or accidents which lead only to death? Listen to David: "If I say, 'Surely the darkness shall cover me; even the night shall be light about me.' Yea, the darkness hideth not from thee; but the night shineth as the day" (Psa. 139:11-12). Once again, our choice can be to cling to Him, to walk with Jesus into the Light of the Resurrection. Who would choose the darkness?

CHAPTER 26

Forest Fires:

A Look at the Dark Side

In the last chapter of reflection, I took a rather romantic look at the darkness of forest fires and other devastation. To be honest, I must take this thought a bit further. In order to truly walk in the Light, we have to deal face-on with the causes of darkness and understand how Jesus can help us walk with Him despite our experiences and our doubts.

One of the saddest experiences of my life came as a result of a visit with one of the dearest people in my life. In my days of studying American literature, one professor was by far my favorite. Under his coaching, I not only learned to understand and care about all of the leading American authors but to love and respect so many of them as varied as Ralph Waldo Emerson, Mark Twain, Ernest Hemingway, and Billy Collins and to write under very high standards myself. I took every course this professor offered, graded freshman papers for him through work-study, and formed a friendship which lasted the rest of his life. The only area we didn't view similarly related to faith, because he was a confirmed atheist

After his wife died, an event which he spoke about very little, I visited him in Helena, Montana, the last time at the assisted living center where he lived his final years. When I arrived for the visit, I found him weepy, depressed, and doing poorly in every way. He finally blurted out that his twin brother had died and he couldn't live without that "other half" of him in the world. Even though I did my best to comfort him and to let him know how important his life was to people like me who loved him, I know his depression lasted for the short time he lived after that visit.

My beloved professor had encountered two major forest fires in his life -- the first his wife's death, which evidently was assuaged some by his children, and the second his twin's death, which obviously burned even harder into his existence. He couldn't find his way out of the darkness because in his mindset, his brother's final destiny was a dark hole in the ground, not eternity in heavenly light. He had no Light of the World to walk beside, to find the seeds of continued existence blooming into new spiritual growth out of tragedy. Although I still grieve for my dear old friend, I can tell you that my belief is stronger because I could see the futility and catastrophe of a lack of Christian faith.

Back to the beautiful new forest brought about by the devastation of the forest fires, I found myself reflecting that day that God's hand is in all things. Our black experiences can be God's way of leading us to new growth. Just as our daughter's friends renewed relationships with siblings because of her devastating loss of her "little brother," we ourselves and those around us can be inspired to have better lives and deeper faith as a result of what we live through. I have read book after book by people who have faced everything from abuse to physical disabilities to psychological trauma and have found their spiritual journey strengthened. Just as the devastated forest floor becomes host to wildflowers and tree seedlings because the light is no longer impeded by tall trees, our lives can become host to great insight and beauty when obstacles to faith are removed.

Is it absurd to see our advantages like health, physical wholeness and prosperity as obstacles to faith? Talk to the people who have begun their travels at the speed of Light because they have lost something crucial in their lives. For myself, I can assure you that the death of our son not only offered new life through transplants for others but also offered to us strengthening of our marriage and our spiritual lives. This is why we are asked by St. Paul to "give God thanks in all things" (1 Thessalonians 5:18).

Some verses in the Bible are tough to deal with, not just for us lay people but for seminary students, ministers and high officials in every church. This verse is tough. Oh, yes, we can give thanks to God for many things, but can we give Him thanks for ALL things? Those forest fires, those tragedies, those sources of darkness? We can give Him thanks in all things only if we understand that no matter what the situation, He is at work in our lives shining Light to dispel the darkness, giving grace to atone for sin, promising eternity in place of death.

CHAPTER 27

Resilience:

The Gritty Side of True Light

"You are God my stronghold. Why have you rejected me? Why must I go about mourning, oppressed by the enemy? Send forth your light and your truth, let them guide me; let them bring me to your holy mountain, to the place where you dwell. Then will I go to the altar of God, to God, my joy and my delight" (Psalm 43:2-4).

As in many of his Psalms, David writes in these prayerful verses about two opposite sides of his existence. He is rejected, in mourning and oppressed. But in just asking God to send forth His light and truth, David finds his spirits lifted and his hopes renewed, his whole being filled with praises. David had discovered a gift generously bestowed on believers: resilience.

Just as we too often attempt to "soften" the hard truths and stories of the Bible, so we often do the same in regard to light. Unless we are stumbling across dunes in the Sahara begging for water, we tend to use soft terms in relation to light. And though the Savior we wish to walk with has His gentle and compassionate side, we need to understand all aspects of His character. Is He the tender Jesus blessing the children or gently healing the blind man, or is He the strong man accosting the moneychangers in the temple, controlling the storm, or calling Lazarus out of the tomb after four days of death? Of course, He is both, and we need to learn from Him in this as in so many things.

The strength which carried Jesus through all of the experiences in the Gospels and at the end up that hill to Golgotha is the strength of resilience. Resilience is not just "bouncing back" or "carrying on"; it is an inner resource which can keep us from the deepest recesses of that black hole, which can give us the ability not only to survive death, disaster and depression but also to emerge on the other side stronger in character and in understanding. Resilience enables us to join Jesus in understanding that when God's will is done, blessings will come from all experiences.

My awareness of the worth and fragility of life, the need for living with respect for every day and every person in it, and the value of conscious love of those around us has increased exponentially. I pray more often, I treasure God's love more deeply, and I thank God in all things. Do these gifts come from me? No, they come from David's God made flesh in the Light of the World who walks beside me as long as I stay committed to walking beside Him.

Let's return to David. When he speaks of his desperation and then his hope, he is not speaking of his own resilience. At that point, he turns entirely to God to find assurance that his life will continue and he can find joy. However, in his faith he is building resilience, the self-assurance which enabled him to win against Goliath and later will enable him to be an unforgettable king. We need to understand that when we walk with Jesus, we not only find answers in His strength but we also build strength of our own. Some of the most powerful people I have ever known are people who have turned their lives over entirely to God. As long as they keep in step with the Light of the World, they are able to be true lights in others' lives.

A perfect illustration of this phenomenon is the growth of the early Christian church. Peter and Paul and the other Apostles found their strength and resilience in their commitment to God through His risen Son, and from that point on they were unstoppable. They went from a tiny group hiding from the Romans to the predominant faith in all of Europe. Are you feeling like Peter or Paul today? Do you need to lead the church for the whole western world? Maybe not – maybe you just need the grit to cope with the losses and challenges in your own life. The same God who inspired them can inspire you. If you do not think you can be that strong, take a deep breath! Why a deep breath? Because "inspire" means "to breathe into," and the same Savior who can give you His Light and His Living Water can breathe into you His strength, which can carry you through all of life and into eternal life.

CHAPTER 28

This Little Light of Mine:
Being Children of Light

The church lies in darkness this night of Christmas Eve, and the people dwell in expectation. Then from somewhere come the words, "The people who walked in darkness have seen a great light," and a single candle is lit by the altar. That beginning is followed by all the wonderful words of Isaiah which welcome the Christ as "Wonderful, Counselor, the Mighty God, the Everlasting Father, the Prince of Peace" (Isaiah 9:6), and one by one, candles are lit along the front of the church and the windows, until this holy place radiates light. No spotlight could manifest this beauty, this warmth, this welcome for the Child.

Our focus up to this point has been Jesus as the Light of the World and our journey with Him. However, as Jesus came to the end of His worldly ministry, He talked to His followers about making the most of His Light, because the day was coming when the Light would no longer be with them and the darkness would return. His words in John 12:35 are, "You are going to have the light just a little while longer. Walk while you have the light, before darkness overtakes you. Whoever walks in the dark does not know where they are going." However, His thought does not end with the darkness. In verse 36 he adds, "Believe in the light while you have the light, so that you may become children of light."

In Matthew 5:14-15, our travels with the Light of the World take us a step further: Now we are the light of the world! "You are the light of the world. A city set on a hill cannot be hidden; nor does anyone light a lamp and put it under a basket, but on the lampstand, and it gives light to all who are in the house...." Notice that we are "the light of the world" without capital letters, simply because our light has to come from Him. I remember a priest gesturing to the beautiful stained glass windows in a church and commenting, "A saint is a person whom the light shines through." Wow! If we are to be part of the "communion of saints" (from the Apostles' Creed), the light has to shine through us – and we can be the light of the world. Then we need to heed His words, to keep our light on the hill or the lampstand rather than hiding it.

What happens to Jesus' followers at the time of Pentecost? They appear to all the people with flames above their heads, flames which represent the power of the Holy Spirit in their lives, flames which carry the Light of the World to all peoples of all times. The power of that Light can be witnessed in the meteoric spread of the early church, moving from hidden rooms in Jerusalem to all of the world traveled by the proclaimers of the Gospel.

Most of us don't have Pentecost-sized flames above our heads. We can admire Saint Peter, Saint Paul, Mother Teresa, Martin Luther King, Norman Vincent Peale, Billy Graham, Sheila Walsh, Charles and Lucy Swindoll, Pope Francis and many others whose individual lights propel them into the "spotlight" and brighten our Christian world. Despite knowing that we can't compete with that kind of light, we can feel Jesus' arm around our shoulders as He reminds us that He isn't asking everyone to light up a national or international pulpit. He is asking for "this little light of mine," the candle flame which makes the difference when the power is out, the gentle light which enables other people to find their way up out of the caves of their darkness. I've seen a little child share a homemade picture and a smile with a nursing home patient and light up that person's face and life. Jesus makes it clear that the child's small light is every bit as important to His kingdom as a Billy Graham Crusade. Does that make Billy Graham's importance to millions less? No, it just reminds us that every person traveling with the Light of the World becomes a conduit of light to the rest of humanity. One of God's "little miracles" is what happens when we share our little light, even in the humblest way like that child in the nursing home. Not only do we light up someone else's world, we find our own world brighter. Unlike the addictions and hatreds and obsessions we have discussed, sharing our light is not self-focused, but in that unselfish moment the Light intensifies in our own lives.

CHAPTER 29

Candelabra:

Little Lights Shining Together

One of my favorite possessions was made for me by my brother as a wedding gift over 40 years ago. Beautifully carved and shaped on a lathe, it has a base of maple, an arched center of juniper, and five candleholders of oak, all polished to shining wood beauty. Five taper candles complete this lovely candelabra, which has decorated my golden oak upright piano, gone with me when I accompanied choral Christmas concerts, and actually served as my evening light for dining and reading during a three-day power outage.

Candelabras, menorahs, and even arrangements of candles provide us with another way to look at light. When we consider the sun or other single sources of light, we realize that they must be intensely powerful in order to provide illumination alone. One "candle power" just can't compare with that kind of power, just as we Christians with "this little light of mine" cannot compare with the power of our Savior as the Light of the World.

However, a candelabra full of candles can provide enough light to illumine a large area. Furthermore, it can provide that light in a way that adds beauty to life as well as a necessary remedy to darkness.

Notice that when Jesus established His church through Peter and the other Apostles, He did not expect any of them to be the light of the world alone or to have all of the power and obligation to make the church work alone. Instead, He counted on the candelabra of followers to provide the light together.

What a variety of candles they were! – some short, some tall, some older, some younger, some as major leaders, some as minor leaders, and some as followers including the many women who provided meals and homey places for gathering together in His name. Some undoubtedly provided steady light and some flickering flames, but the result of their collective efforts and faith was a church which would spread throughout the known world and within a few generations become the official church of the whole Roman Empire. That takes a lot of candles!

I am sure you know people who insist that they don't need to attend church because their faith is individual. The answer to that concept is that Jesus worked with a group of followers to establish a church because individual faith is only one candle against the darkness. Collective faith not only creates the greater light of the candelabra but also provides reason to keep burning, to keep being part of the light. In addition, churches are led by people who study and dedicate themselves to an understanding of how to value and intensify the light. The best ministers, priests and lay leaders I have known are those who love the Light of the World and love each follower no matter the size of the flame.

One more important factor affecting our little lights is that candles don't burn on their own. It takes a match or a lighter, some source of flame beyond the power of the candle itself. None of us can just spontaneously ignite but instead must turn to the Light of the World and ask for the power to burn for Him. A prayer of repentance, a prayer of belief, a prayer of dedication to the Light, and your candle will be lit, ready to join the candelabra of Christians around you. What a beautiful moment that is!

Perhaps you have already experienced the moment of beginning your walk with the Light of the World. Make sure that smothering sin or gusts of indifference don't extinguish your flame. As I have mentioned so many times, truly walking with Jesus, talking to Him, and listening to and reading His word can ensure that your little light will continue to be part of the candelabra which can light your home, your workplace, your church, your neighborhood and anywhere else you shine.

Imagine the time when the Romans were most horribly persecuting Christians and Peter was forced to meet with followers in the labyrinth caves under part of the city. Fear and darkness surrounded the people who sought this refuge. However, they found in those dark caves the light of Peter's presence and words, combined with the faith each of them had growing within him or her. That candelabra would light the fledgling church through its earliest days and eventually sustain it even after the death of Peter. We should never doubt the power of little lights banded together to follow the Light.

CHAPTER 30

Radiance around Us:

People whom the Light Shines Through

I have mentioned the priest who referred one Sunday to the Saints in the beautiful stained glass windows around the church, warmly lit by the morning sun and told us that a Saint is" a person whom the light shines through," and we are all part of the "communion of saints." Made in God's image, we are endowed with His Light, given from before birth the gift of His knowing and His radiance.

Each human being contains that radiance, something you can see shining out of the eyes of a newborn baby, a happy child, a devoted mother or father, a friend, or anyone who cares about you. If you are genuinely in love, I can guarantee that you can bask in that light in your loved one's eyes, and that lovelight never dims as long as it is shared. Suffering from severe macular degeneration and dementia -- seeing only shadows both physically and mentally -- my mother still showed that lovelight whenever she was close to my father. The next time you are alone with a family member or friend, take a moment to view that light in them and from them. You will find that their flaws become unimportant and their worth in your life and the lives of others around them becomes extremely important.

Jesus and His Light can gift you with amazing friendships. At one point, I had let my life drift far from my solid Christian roots, and I was making choices which would have appalled my parents and undoubtedly appalled my God. A package arrived from my dear friend Roseanne with a simple note, "I have a feeling that you need this. It has been blessed by the archbishop in Denver." Inside on a chain was a beautiful pewter medal of Mary cradling Jesus, a strong reminder not only of my Christian faith but also of my dream to someday be a wife and mother. Such a woman would not want to be affected by the physical or emotional fallout caused by poor life choices. That simple gesture by a Christian friend put my life back on track.

My closest friend Sue inspires me constantly, partly because she is literally tuned into "the peace that passes all understanding." We retired together, have fun together, and so often think in tandem – but those things could be true of non-Christian friends. The major difference is that I know she prays for me and will always listen with God's will in mind. Many friends were kind when Josh died, but Sue was essential. Her faith and friendship are so bonded that I could know that Jesus was sharing His Light through her and that I never need to worry about overtaxing either the friendship or the Light. Who are the Sues in your life, the people whom the Light shines through? Are you taking them for granted, forgetting to thank God for them and to return the Light?

Some "lights of the world" appear in unexpected places and ways. When I graduated from college in 1970, I moved to New York for a year, about as far from my roots in Montana as one can get. I found a church to be part of and volunteered for youth leadership. A perky retired schoolteacher named Marion heard me singing with the kids and invited me to be part of the adult choir, and soon I was surrounded by friends making "a joyful noise unto the Lord." I only saw Marion twice more before her death at age 93. But we are Christian friends, endowed with God's Light, destined for eternity not only with Jesus but with each other.

I strongly believe that we are created to be sunny, to live with optimism and intensity, but we cannot do that if we are turned only inward. Not long after Josh's burial, I was at home one cold evening when my husband was gone, and my world was very bleak. A knock at the door revealed dear friends who had driven 15 miles with a stockpot of homemade chicken soup and bread. As we sat down together to feast, my darkness dissolved in the light of their kindness. The look on their faces told me that their world was lighter, too, as a result of the light they shared. I can still picture that evening and taste that wonderful soup.

Imagine how the eyes of our loved ones will gleam when they see us joining them in Heaven. We're all going to shine, shine, shine!

✦ *PART VI* ✦

LIGHT THROUGHOUT OUR LIVES

CHAPTER 31

Sunrises and Sunsets:

Births and Deaths

I writhe with each contraction, eyes whisking, searching for some solace but met with the sterility of white walls and white lights. At the periphery of both my sight and my hearing, a doctor works with obtrusive hands to turn the child, but the tsunamic waves are too strong.

Now the room buzzes with voices and clattering, commanding me to breathe, to push, to hold back, to continue the battle. The large breech baby begins to emerge, hips followed by legs folded tight against the sides of his torso, until only his shoulders and head remain inside. The danger increases as the cord is closed off. I rise up and almost scream into the white lights as a final spasm sends my boy into waiting hands, ready to clear his throat and nose. My husband's intense eyes hold mine through the lights, waiting for what seems an eternity. Then a loud cry from Josh, and the lights are full of rainbows.

One of God's most light-filled promises is that He knows us before our births and continues to know us for the rest of eternity. Just as the sunrise holds the promise of the day, so each baby's birth holds the promise of life everlasting. How sad that we live in a society

which finds babies disposable and objects of abuse and neglect --
God's lights literally hidden under a bushel or extinguished by the
sabre of selfishness and godlessness. As Christians, one of the most
vital things we can do to remain in the Light is to value babies and
little children and to pray that our country and our society return to
doing so.

I included rainbows along with Josh's birth because rainbows
are a biblical reminder that God keeps His promises made in His
covenants. The original rainbow came after the Great Flood, a symbol
of God's promise never to destroy mankind again. Every time the
golden light creeps over the horizon, heralded by reds, oranges or
pinks, it renews not only our part of the earth but also God's promise
that our people and our environment will continue as he created
them.

Sunsets are a little different. The light is just as beautiful, often
breathtaking, and in the "Big Sky Country" of Montana, people extol
sunsets as gifts. However, we all know that the waning of the light
will lead, no matter how peacefully, to dusk and darkness. Just as we
revel in the goldenness of autumn yet regret its brevity and its segue
into winter, so also we know that a sunset will be followed by night.
So also we know that the later years of each life are segueing into the
moment of death.

However, for the Christian death is only an end to a life in this
world. Furthermore, death is not really darkness but instead a moment
of travel into the light of eternity, into the presence of the Light of
the World. If we have been walking with Him all along, this moment
consists of major steps, but steps just the same. The Light which was
with us from before our births continues with us without flickering.
Those who see the possibility of the sunrise in each sunset understand
the circular nature of creation and understand how our new life in
Heaven is a renewal of the life we have had in Him forevermore.

What about those left behind? We need to remember that the separation is only temporary and the person still exists despite being beyond our vision. After Josh's death, my granddaughter Parker gazed at her mother and said, "You used to have two brothers; now you only have one." "No," my daughter wisely replied, "I still have two brothers – one on earth and one in Heaven." Thus, when we sense a loved one's presence despite death, we are truly experiencing the continued light of that person's life as it shines in our present just as it shone in our past. The loss is only physical – not an easy component but nevertheless greatly overshadowed by the perpetual light.

I picture Jesus in the dawn of our lives, inviting us as little children to "come onto Me" and begin our walks which were promised in birth and perhaps in baptism. I picture Him again in the sunset of our lives, perhaps walking beside us in suffering and reassuring us that He truly understands what suffering is all about. However our death comes, He and His Light stay by our sides, for once this walk begins, it never ends. Hallelujah!

CHAPTER 32

Teenage Light Years:

Guidance in the Light

Excerpts from a photo album: They are strong and eager, this trio of teenagers who smile my way in the picture as they shoulder heavy packs. My two sons and daughter are as skittish as race horse colts to take the trail into the Teton wilderness. Grinning into the camera are Clint, the 16-year-old long-distance runner whose humor and spirit will sustain us for five days; Anne, the rangy 14-year-old tennis champion whose intelligence and resilience take well to the long hike; and Josh, the lanky 12-year-old who has almost begged for this day and will relish every adventure.

At the base of the trail five days later, we all pose for the final snapshot. Despite dirty faces and disheveled hair, we are warmly together, arms around each other, grinning into the scene as though we owned the whole park and its secrets. Behind us, sixty-five miles of trails, creeks and waterfalls, wildflowers galore, and the adventure of our lifetimes hold court beneath twelve royal peaks. Only our memories remain, other than hot showers and a steak supper to send us home to lives enriched by the shared escapade. In the ensuing years, many pictures will capture experiences with my beloved children and eventually their families, but none will outshine this backpack trip for freedom, passion and joy.

I share these excerpts from a memoir I wrote because I have always felt such oneness with my Lord in Grand Teton National Park and I treasure having shared that wonderland with my teenagers. Kids are such a special gift to all of us, whether we raise them or teach them or pastor them or have any other roles in their lives, however simple. Spending time with them and sharing our walk with the Light of the World is as essential to their lives as it is to ours.

I have read many accounts of the lives of prisoners-of-war in horrible camps where they have shared their experiences of using memorized Bible verses and prayer to keep themselves not only alive but sane. Can you imagine anything darker than lying in a cell with no bathroom facilities, no decent food, vermin and rodents, and worst of all, no light? Yet these people speak of the darkness being dispelled by God's Word. How sad that one manifestation of the misdirection of our modern society is that so many children are not learning that life-sustaining and light-sustaining Word by heart. What do they have to cling to in the darkest circumstances? The suicide rate not only among teens and young adults but also among preteens attests to the fact that many do not see themselves with anything they can cling to.

The healthier part of our society emphasizes family as the answer for security and sustenance. But what if that support is unavailable for some reason, temporarily or permanently? We know that situations exist where parents die, where family does not support us, where friends desert us, where all of the things we have learned to depend on – job, money, home, good health – are gone. In that terrible darkness, we can lose our selves in every way possible, including the consideration or possibly the act of taking our own lives.

What do our young adults need the most? New electronic gadgets, their own cell phones for "security," more of everything, assurances that family will always be with them? No, they need that stripped-down figure on the Cross, that Lord with nothing left including His own robe. The young people – and adults – of our world need to know that they are loved so deeply that Jesus was willing to give up everything to die and to journey to Hell in atonement for their sins. He emerged from that grave offering eternal life, the most glorious future that anyone can imagine.

No one with experience around teenagers will claim that those years are easy. But if we see each one as a child of God in need of the Light, then we can realize that even if the steps are in different rhythms, the walk and the destiny are the same. Just as I shared those mountain trails, we need to encourage teens to walk at the speed of Light all their lives, and we need to enlist every bit of help to make sure that their lives are not lives of darkness but lives where the Light is always present. From baptism to confirmation to adult commitment, each child-become-teenager-become-adult needs our support, love and prayers no matter what rocks mar their trails.

CHAPTER 33

Shadows:

Divisions which Disrupt the Light

From the beginning, this book has been based on the revelations I have experienced as a result of the death of someone dear followed by travels through grief enlightened by walking with the Lord. Together we have looked at many sources of darkness, both those that happen to us and those that happen because of our choices, and we have seen that Jesus' Light shines through if we embrace His presence and Word. Walking with Him is serious business turned into joy, but in between the choice and the joy can lie many stumbling blocks.

One thing we learn from the experiences of the Disciples as they walked with Jesus through His ministry is that even the most dedicated group instituted by the Messiah when He called them to be "fishers of men" will have its times of division. These men who later would base their total lives and eventually their deaths on belief in the Light of the World spent part of their time with Jesus staggering astray. They doubted Him, they missed vital points like asking the women not to bother the tired Jesus with their children when He wanted them to come to Him and learn of Him. They argued among themselves as to who would be top dog in the Kingdom. They did not listen when He spoke of His death and Resurrection and later paid dearly in grief and confusion until they learned that He was no longer in the tomb and then saw Him.

From the Disciples to our church congregations and committees as well as groups like my college Campus Ministry, petty or major disagreements, resentments, misinterpretations and actual wrongs can mar the journey in the Light. The same shadows that cause divisions in what Elton Trueblood called "the company of the committed" can plague our marriages, family relationships and friendships. How can we walk together with the Light of the World when we are in the shadows?

The first answer to that question lies in ourselves. The reason that Jesus harshly called on His followers to forsake their families and friends – actually their total former existences – was that He knew the first steps in a strong, steady walk with Him must be taken with only the role of a follower in mind. The beginning of our walk may be started or influenced by others, but we cannot have a group relationship with the Lord if we do not have a strong individual relationship with Him. When I was teaching, I talked to students a lot about focus. Whether they were pursuing academic studies, learning to sing or play instruments, or pursuing various sports, nothing would go well without commitment, responsibility, and above all, focus. Jesus often spoke of that need for individual focus and faith with people like the Samaritan woman at the well. He amazed her with His knowledge of her personal life, He presented her with His living water, and only then did He strengthen her by enabling her to share with others.

The second answer comes from study of the Scriptures and understanding of what needs to happen in our relationships with others. Faith demands sharing, receiving demands giving, leading demands serving, and the toughest answer comes when forgiveness demands forgiving. Jesus illustrated each one of these with parables and His own example. Can you imagine the Disciples' reaction when Jesus gathered them into the room for the Last Supper and first acted as a servant to wash their feet? We have, of course, Peter's reaction – he wanted more and had to be reminded again to follow – but they all must have been astonished and deeply affected by that act.

The shadows in our walk come most often from relationships skewed by wrongs and lack of forgiveness. Our sense of justice takes over, and we are sure that we cannot forgive because it is not fair. Perhaps we are angry, perhaps we are hurt, and suffering magnifies unfairness. However, God's justice is different than our perceptions. How "fair" was it to hang an innocent man on a cross because mankind was sinful? Forgiveness, then, cannot arise from a sense of justice but from a sense of God's will and Jesus' words and ways. As human beings, we walk heavily, burdened down not only by our own guilt but by our lack of forgiveness. The only way to lighten our loads and our steps is to accept grace for our guilt and forgiveness in exchange for forgiving others. Jesus walks with light steps. Can we?

CHAPTER 34

Sundial:

When Life Needs Organization and Direction

Fresh out of college and headed to the East Coast by train for adventure, I had a layover of several hours in Chicago. My father suggested that I spend the time at the Museum of Science and Industry and the Adler Planetarium. Wow! The exhibits at the museum were beyond anything I had ever imagined, and the planetarium affected me like a magician's wand. Spellbound, I almost forgot to return to the train station. Although I sailed through the stars with abandonment, an exhibit of ancient sundials inflated my wonder even more.

Sundials, which vary by century and by origin around the world, tell time and date by the sun yet depend upon a piece called a gnomon to cast a shadow so that the sundial can be read. That description amuses me because in my extolling of the Light I have cautioned about the shadows, yet in this case the shadow is essential. Let us pause for thought along that line. What is the purpose of the sundial? Very simply, to indicate time and day to enable people to order their lives not only by the seasons but by the movement of the sun. Can we learn something from the sundial?

Spiritual lives need order just as physical and mental lives do. We know, for example, that class schedules in schools are geared to offering the curriculum in a way that optimizes learning, considering such things as attention spans, time needed for everything from chemistry labs to band practices, and appropriate times for breaks and lunches. Religious communities such as convents and monasteries apply those same principles, making sure that work and rest are intermingled with prayer, meditation and worship in a way that maximizes devotion and spiritual growth. Long ago, people in communities would hear bells calling them to prayer including matins in the morning and vespers in the evening. The day was literally bordered with religious devotion.

Now we are living in a time when schedules are paramount yet pertain only to our work or school, our needs like meals, and our play. Where does our spiritual life fit into all of this? We need to be aware that when we are living lives by schedules, if we do not include spiritual things, they will not happen. Families who regularly attend church services plus such events as Bible studies and Sunday School or Confirmation classes have to make those things a priority in their schedules or they will be swallowed up by the greedy jaws of modern society. In addition, each of us needs some time for study, reflection and prayer.

Let us return to my comment about the sundial's dependence upon the shadow of the gnomon to enable use of the sun to order lives. Can we use awareness of the shadows in our lives to trigger making time for the Light of the World? If we are truly going to walk with Him, then we have to make time to read His words, to talk to Him, and to listen to Him. Obviously, those things should happen daily but also when we most need them. My spiritual life increased in regularity as I emerged from the darkest sea of grief, and the more my shadows indicated my need, the more I reached out and clung to the lifesaver of Jesus' Light, comfort and peace.

Notice that the awareness of shadows and light could not come until I had come out of the total darkness. Sundials do not work at night! Lives immersed in depression do not respond to the order, schedules, and focus I have advocated. The creator of a sundial has to have total faith in the fact that night will end and the sun will rise and shine. So we, too, need faith in the fact that the Light of the World is always there and our darkness can end to the extent that we can get on with re-establishing order and focus. That puts the shadows in their place!

I have mentioned our friend who was a strong leader in Alcoholics Anonymous. Among other profound pieces of guidance, he admonished members to order their lives around their spiritual needs, to make sure that meetings and other opportunities for help and healing were priorities. Their shadows guided their twelve steps on their spiritual journeys, and their faith kept them in the presence of the Light. I envision our friend pointing to the sundial, reminding his colleagues that each day is a new walk with the Savior and His saving Grace.

CHAPTER 35

Holiday Lights:

Dealing with an Un-Merry Christmas

Every year our house nearly burst at the seams during the holidays from Thanksgiving through New Year's Day. We gathered often, sometimes at different times following my mother's thought that holidays together are important but we can celebrate whenever family is able to come.

Every gathering was full of laughter, full of music and dancing, full of generosity, and full of eating wonderful meals prepared by skilled hands. Notice that the common word is "full" and always led to happiness. A house full of precious people literally "fulfills" our ideal of family and holidays.

Fast forward to the present. One chair is permanently empty. Fullness and fulfilled-ness are an impossibility because Josh is dead and his widow has understandably moved on although she is always welcome. Can we still gather and celebrate? Of course. Will it ever be the same with a "full" family and the ideal intact? Never.

Grief over losses and sadness over our own challenges can unplug the holiday lights. One absent loved one acts like that single missing bulb that stops the entire string from lighting up. When the light goes out of the holidays, no amount of feasting or gathering can bring back the merry, and people who have lost family members can tell you that holiday grief is more intense than everyday grief because of the intensity of the memories.

My memories take me back to a Christmas at Josh's house, and I can still hear his laughter over the kids and the gifts. The pictures pop out of the album: Josh setting his 3-year-old nephew on the neck of the elk mounted on his wall, Josh playing tag with all the kids, Josh patting a full stomach and grinning at his sister offering pie, Josh hugging us tight as we left, not knowing that treasured time would be the last Christmas with him.

How do we who suffer wrap ourselves in the plush blanket of Christmas warmth when we are wrapped in frigid darkness? How do we see candlelight clearly through tears? How do we decorate a Christmas tree or a Christmas table when red and green has faded to grey? How do we gather together when the gathering does not include everyone we were sure would always be there?

The answer we can reach for is a change of focus, turning our mental cameras away from the empty chair and toward the source of Light who is the source of the holiday. Think about the things which Mary "pondered in her heart" after Jesus' early days, knowing that within the glorious hallelujahs of the birth of the Messiah was the prediction of His death. The Child in the manger would die, but in dying He would overcome the darkness.

Whether we are observing Thanksgiving by giving thanks to God for our many blessings, observing Christmas by gathering and sharing in Jesus' name, or observing the New Year by looking forward to another year of God's presence in our lives, we can focus on the Light of the World and His power to overcome death and darkness. He will wrap His loving arms around every gathering and every hurting soul.

The important things are to avoid rejecting the holidays and to avoid allowing grief to isolate us at a time when we need others. Remember that when Jesus walked on earth, he focused on the people and their needs for hope and understanding. We can walk at the speed of Light during the holidays by following His example, reaching out, offering hope and giving generously to those who need our love. Read the scriptures, find a kindred soul to pray with, attend a religious service, and warm your hands and heart at the hearth fire of Jesus' Love and Light.

Through all of this, honor your memories of your missing loved ones. View the pictures, tell the stories, observe the traditions which meant a lot to them. Part of our ache over Josh is that he will never celebrate another holiday, and I know that others feel the same thing about their missing parent, spouse, sibling, child, or friend. Again, if our focus is on walking with Jesus, He will remind us that each of these people celebrated holidays and now are celebrating eternal life with Him. Thanksgiving turns to singing His praises in Heaven, Christmas turns to the presence of the Prince of Peace, and each New Year becomes embracing eternity.

Oh, come, Emanuel, and ransom souls captive in darkness. You are our blessed Light of the holidays and always.

✦*PART VII*✦

LIGHT THROUGHOUT
OUR WORLD

CHAPTER 36

Light of Joy:
Good News in the Pursuit of Happiness

My youngest son is dead, my father to whom I was so close died three months after my son, other family concerns are troubling, and neuropathy keeps me combatting constant pain. Friends have asked me how I can seem happy, because I can manage to view life with some optimism despite all this, to take delight in people, events, music, literature, special projects, writing, and many other things.

The answer is not in happiness. Happiness requires a cause, always something ephemeral. We can be happy because we get a job, because someone loves us, because we have money to spend, because we have our health, because we get a gift. All of those things are legitimate, but they take happiness with them if they fail or disappear. If we do not get the job or it turns sour, if someone dies or leaves us, if we run short of money, if our health fails, if the gift is lost or broken, happiness turns to sadness. No wonder we feel at times as if we were living life on an emotional rollercoaster, with exhilaration constantly brought down by anguish.

The answer is in Joy. Joy is a gift of God, beginning with glorious angel song and the marveling of shepherds, common people like most of us. God offers us Joy through the life and Resurrection of His Son, a gift which goes hand-in-hand with Grace. Joy comes to us through belief, exclusive of those things which can come and go in our lives. Joy allows my husband and me to praise His name even in our grief because we know that eternal life is ours just as it is our son's. Nothing can take away that Joy – not death, not unemployment, not poverty, not sickness, and especially not lack of material things. Does that mean that we are unrealistic, bobbing along on some sort of fluffy cloud while ignoring the difficulties and wrongs in the world? Of course not. We gasp at the ups and downs of the rollercoaster like everyone else. However, we are not dependent on the rollercoaster and can find the "peace that passes all understanding" by reveling in the Joy which is God's gift.

The American Declaration of Independence states that our rights include life, liberty and the pursuit of happiness. Notice that the right is not happiness itself but the pursuit of happiness. Jefferson and the signers of that document wanted a nation which offered all of us the chance to find happiness through work, family, adventure, or whatever appeals to us. How wonderful that "pursuit" can be! And most of us find some degree of happiness in families, job successes and accomplishments.

What about those who fail in the pursuit of happiness, through their own fault or through unforeseen changes? How many sink into the quicksand of grief and despair? How many turn even further to escape through substance abuse, promiscuity, gambling, acts of desperation, and sometimes the total escape of suicide? How futile is it to remind these people that they have the right to the pursuit of happiness? The paralysis of grief and death and the darkness of life without hope can halt that pursuit dismally. In those circumstances, even life and liberty seem like rights with no substance.

God's Joy can change all that. Joy comes with built-in radiance, light for our way from the Light of the World. Does that mean that we can just tell ourselves or others to embrace Joy and get over the lack of happiness? No, the first step is not to start a pursuit of Joy but instead to turn to faith in God and Jesus. The first tear in the canopy of darkness comes when we recognize our despair and pain and pray for God's help. Only He can send a beam through that tear and remind us that His Son offers not only Light but Joy

Because Joy is born of God and rooted in Him, it is always present and always renewable. We can continue to pursue happiness, to look for solutions to sadness. However, if our foundation is Joy, we can live with the times when happiness is elusive. Like a David Copperfield show, where "reality" is based on illusion, we have times when happiness can disappear, "Poof!" Joy, however, sits beside us in the audience and remains our constant companion as long as we believe in the source of Joy, the gentle Savior who asks only that we turn our pursuit into the only journey that really matters.

CHAPTER 37

Light of Joy:
Pursuing the Gift

People who experience darkness through grief, addiction, fear, bad health or other causes can tell you that the darkness never goes away permanently. We can seem to overcome grief or addiction, cope with fear and challenges, but the darkness lurks like some monster in the closet, ready to burst out like a child's nightmare and extinguish the light. Every time that threat looms, we need to go to the Creator and the Prince of Peace as our source of Joy, realizing that the Joy was never extinguished just as the darkness was never extinguished. That is the true gift of Joy, that it exists no matter how much darkness we encounter, no matter how we fail in our pursuit of happiness, no matter how desperate we feel.

Let me suggest that when we pray, after we pray for God's mercy and Jesus' compassion, we need to pray less for the solutions to our problems and more for the awareness of Joy. Then having recognized the source of our Joy, we need to be aware of reminders of Joy throughout our existence. Babies' smiles, friends' laughter, nature's beauties, all of those things of all sizes can radiate that Joy. I have a friend who has been through cancer treatment twice and a connected miscarriage, lost her husband when he couldn't cope, lost a brother to suicide, and is watching her mother succumb to Alzheimer's. So what does she do to combat all that darkness? In her faith and inner Joy, she reaches out to others by working every afternoon at a women's shelter. You should see the smile she bestows on the women and children while she serves them meals and attends to their needs! That smile does not come from the pursuit of happiness; it comes from Joy.

Other than from prayer and awareness of little things, how do we embrace Joy in our daily existence despite the constant presence of challenges? First, we can follow my friend's example because reaching out to others spreads the Joy. Remember the smile on Jimmy Stewart's face as well as the smiles of everyone else at the party at the end of *It's a Wonderful Life*? While "Hark, the Herald Angels Sing" is shared by all of these people of faith, Joy shines from all of them as a result of caring for each other and giving generously despite hard times.

One fall a group of us members of the Daughters of the American Revolution volunteered for a day with Habitat for Humanity. I was interested in the organization because it thrives and proves that nourishing hope and pride in people needing a hand up works far better than throwing tax money at the problem, and I figured that our reward would be awareness of a job well done. The awareness did come, particularly after we learned to cut and lay sod. But the reward was far different.

I worked with an older man whose daughter and three children were living with him in his tiny quarters with only two beds. One of the children, a teenager, laid sod with me and talked about her life and how many years she had longed and prayed for a real home. Every time she paused to look toward the house which was close to being ready for her family, her face would literally shine. What I was witnessing was Joy, flowing over and swirling around all of us. Of course, she was happy about the house, but her Joy went much deeper because Jesus had been beside her through the dark years to the sun-filled days when her prayers were being answered.

Second, we can reach out for that help ourselves when needed. I have mentioned a few times a special friend who celebrated his nearly 20 years of sobriety by heading an Alcoholics Anonymous chapter and working hard to assist others with alcohol-free lives. The people of all ages who reached out to him found help not only to stop drinking but to turn to God for deeper faith and deeper Joy. Groups and Christian-based counseling exist not only for substance abuse but also for grief, depression, and darknesses of all kinds. One of my dearest friends is a minister who experienced suicide in her family and now offers insight and solace to anyone dealing with such tragedy. She not only has Joy but shares it. Find someone like her when you are troubled. Reach out to that person, absorb the answers, and then embrace the Joy. And don't forget to thank God.

CHAPTER 38

Meteor Showers:

When Faith Takes Our Breath Away

The young Girl Scout campers are in bed, and my friend and I, relieved for the night from our counselor duties, amble up the familiar trail to the top of Boulder Hill. Settling in to our usual comfortable spot, we opt to forego the usual little campfire just because this is a special August night. I treasure these times. We are always comfortably in tune, whether chatting about frivolous or serious issues or just being silent. Loving the wilderness is as important in these summers together in the Montana mountains as loving the children we are guiding to that same love.

Together we draw in delighted breaths as the sky explodes in shooting stars, far more spectacular than man-made fireworks. NASA will tell you that these shooting stars, in groups called meteor showers, are actually a matter of the earth's orbit going through the fragments left from a comet trail. Two of those meteor showers, the Delta Aquarids and the Perseids, happen around the same time in August, although the Perseids are the ones which put on the brightest show.

Because God created our minds to encompass not only scientific exploration and knowledge but also a sense of beauty and wonder, we can delve into the nature of the Perseids as we gaze with awe at the brilliance of the sky. Walt Whitman wrote a perceptive poem about hearing the "learn'd astronomer" with all his scientific details and then leaving the lecture room to go outside, where he "look'd up in perfect silence at the stars." Whitman has a point; yet there should be no reason why scientific knowledge should eclipse wonder and appreciation.

The subject of meteor showers – grand displays of light as opposed to tiny glimmers – takes us to the subject of conversion. From the Greek for "turning with," conversion is a term long used by theologians to describe the moment at which a person accepts belief; in the Christian religion, it is the moment often described as "accepting Jesus into your heart." Conversion is the moment when by "turning with" the Light of the World, we begin our walk in the Light. For many people like me, I slipped seamlessly into the garment of Light as a child in Sunday School, knowing that the faith of my parents was what I believed. That faith had to be nurtured and strengthened, of course, but nevertheless it was always there like a single steady star.

However, many people experience their turning toward the Light in different ways and degrees. A meteor shower-style revelation burst upon one of the most influential characters in the Bible, Saul of Tarsus who would become St. Paul. Saul was deliberately dwelling in darkness, adamant in his hatred and persecution of Christians based upon misdirected "faith." Doesn't that strike a chord in modern times? Then God literally struck him blind with the intensity of His Light, and when Saul emerged, he was a different man. He was no longer on the road to Damascus, intent on his own itinerary, but literally propelled onto roads to places all over that part of the world where he would bring the Light to the Gentiles and write so much of our Bible.

Do we know why God sends a major star to wise men and shepherds, a meteor-bright light to people like St. Paul, a steady glowing star to many others? No, but we are reminded that God's ways are not our ways, that much is beyond our understanding. What we do know is that light is always involved and that moments of enlightenment, like the Transfiguration of Jesus, are to be taken seriously. The result, no matter what the source, must be "turning with" Jesus, walking with Him, absorbing the Light of His presence.

I return to that night on Boulder Hill with my friend, and I see clearly one more gift of that night. A sense of wonder is vital to us all. Little children begin their lives with a sense of wonder, and unfortunately many factors in the "real" world combine to extinguish or at least damage that sense. We all need to get it back and to bask in its light. We need to look up at the night sky and let it take our breath away. That sense of wonder and beauty is part of who we are, gifted by our Creator. At the moment that we let our sense of wonder overwhelm us, we enter into the presence and power of God.

CHAPTER 39

The Ripple Effect:
Taking the Tiniest Step

Water laps around my shoulders in a pristine little lake in eastern Montana as I stand immersed in the coolness of the water and in the loveliness of the late afternoon sky. Sunshine reflects from each tiny wave on the lake's surface. Suddenly, a small fish leaps for a bug and dives back into the lake. Where he reenters the water, a tiny circle radiates out, then another and another. The sunlight dances from ring to ring until that part of the lake is filled with concentric ripples reflecting the light. Eventually I remember to breathe.

As I have mentioned before, when we walk with Jesus at the speed of Light, we never walk alone. In dealing with our own darkness and soaking up our own needed light, we can forget others temporarily, but the Lord of Light reminds us over and over that His Light is shared. Two things are essential: that Jesus be the source of the Light and that others be the sharers of the Light. That little fish in the lake was going about his own business, unaware that I was watching or that other parts of the lake were even involved beyond where his bug flew. However, his action caused the ripple effect which shared rings of light with a large area. When Jesus called the fishermen like Peter,

Andrew, James and John to be "fishers of men," he was not talking simply about reeling in one at a time or throwing out nets for little groups but also about reaching out to all people.

No one understood the ripple effect better than St. Paul. Paul traveled here and there among the Gentile cities, jumping in quickly -- one small fish taking action in each place, depending upon Jesus' Light to move out from that center to enlighten individual after individual and group after group. Many of his letters (epistles) are written to nourish the spreading of the Light and also to stop any darkening impediments which interfere with the natural increase of rings of Light. Paul kept reminding leaders that if the focus is not the Light of the World, each ring no longer has its center of reference, its reason for being. Rings without light can spread the darkness, too.

One of the major tenets of Alcoholics Anonymous is that no one can deal successfully with addiction without realizing the need, committing to the solution, and recognizing the fact that others are there to help and all are taking the journey together. Leaders in AA shine not only through hard-earned wisdom but also through compassion which encircles each person who comes to a meeting and joins the effort. The ripple effect is established when each member knows that someone will help and that someone else needs help. What goes around definitely comes around if the group is to be effective.

Another great example of the ripple effect is the outreach of Heifer International, a worldwide group my family and I love to support. Donors pay for a milk cow heifer, a goat, a sheep – perhaps a whole herd – or a hive of honeybees, a flock of chicks or ducks, or a support system like a good water well. The recipients are trained in agricultural production and then enjoy the benefits of food to eat or products to sell to help with their family's living expenses, education, etc. The project would be good if it stopped right there, but what makes it great is that each recipient is obligated to share the riches. The first female calf from that milk cow, for example, must go to another needy family in the village. Hence, the ripple effect spreads the prosperity through the entire village and beyond.

Jesus never intended that His Light reach only His immediate followers but instead that it reach everyone. The phenomenal growth of the early church despite persecution bears witness to the strength of His message and His Light and the wonder of the ripple effect. Early leaders like Peter and Paul were so enthusiastic that they sent out whole waves that inundated the known world and eventually became the "law of the land." Notice that the success of the spread of Christianity was not a result of some huge tsunami from God but instead a result of ripples from every believer inspired by Jesus' word and example. You and I each doing our small part can increase the ripples of Light and the beauties of God's love in lives all around us.

CHAPTER 40

Lights of Enlightenment:

Illumination in the Fine Arts

S urrounded by other students from the music departments of my college and a neighboring college, I tune up my viola and prepare for our recital concert in the hall where a fairly large crowd waits. We know this music well after weeks of practice, but all of us, including our director, are still dependent upon our music. Then the hall lights are dimmed, and we turn on the tiny lights attached to our music stands. These little lights are well designed, barely even discernable to the audience but providing all the glow we need to see our music well.

Like the stand lights, gifts of enlightenment have been provided by God to brighten our world. The study of aesthetics will show you that human beings have a great need for beauty, not as vital a need as that for water and food but extraordinarily important to good lives. How wonderful that our Creator provided us not only with a natural world full of beauty but also with talents in music, visual arts, drama and composition to make our human world even more beautiful. Of course, sometimes these talents are misused, with results which are anything but beautiful; however, I believe the positive results of such talents far outweigh the negative. Often the positive uses of talent come because artists understand that their talents can be used to glorify the Lord. Imagine how Jesus must smile when those walking with Him reflect His Light in their music, art works, photographs and compositions!

Our stand lights aiding in our music performance are not the only use of light in art. Think about how dependent any dramatic performance is upon stage lights and spotlights. In studying art history and technique, students learn that a principal consideration in art is light – where it comes from and how it is manifest in the work. Artists as different as Johannes Vermeer and Thomas Kinkade are known specifically for their use of light. Photographers like Ansel Adams and Eliot Porter work with light in all its aspects every time a shutter opens.

When my brother and I were working for the National Park Service in Yellowstone National Park in the late 1960's, we had the privilege of singing in choruses with directors and soloists brought in by the Christian Ministry in the National Parks and employed by Hamilton Stores. We performed Handel's *Messiah* at the Old Faithful Inn, Lake Lodge, Canyon Motor Lodge, and the Mammoth Hot Springs Hotel around the 25th of August during the celebration of "Christmas in Yellowstone." My lifetime love of that inspired music has continued through years of my brother's conducting it with the St. Croix Valley Orchestra in Minnesota and years of my singing the "Hallelujah Chorus" with the local Forsyth Community Choir. The Light of God shines through Handel's amazing composition and brings Light to all who hear it.

A dear friend of mine died after a long, painful battle with cancer, the kind of death no one would choose. Before that death she was an amazing teacher, a lovely friend, a gracious mother and grandmother, and beyond that a talented singer with a soprano voice which would raise our Community Choir's rendition of the "Hallelujah Chorus" into a heavenly realm. To this day I can close my eyes and hear her sing "It is Well with My Soul." She walked with the Light of the World with a strong and steady faith and it indeed was well with her soul, even through the time of cancer and death. People like her are so inspiring because she was successful in so many areas of her life but at the same time she stayed in step with Jesus so that He could share her burden and light her way through the darkness and into His kingdom.

What gifts of enlightenment do you have – or, lacking such talent yourself, what gifts can you encourage in loved ones? Like my friend, we need to remember that innate gifts are a blessing of God no matter how they are used, but when those gifts are used as part of our walk with Jesus in His Light, they become a reflection of Him and a far greater gift to the artist as well as the world. Meanwhile, all of us walking at the speed of Light need to seek the light in all things beautiful, whether that light is shining through trees and on mountain tops or whether it is shining through fine arts creations.

CHAPTER 41

Sparkles of Joy:

The Light in Nature

Light dances on the ripples of Rock Creek, my favorite trout stream beneath the grandeur of the Beartooth Mountains in south central Montana. Sunbeams penetrate this clear water, painting with a soft patina the multi-colored granite rocks in the riverbed. Eternity flows, clothed in the light, beckoning not only to the fisherman like my brother but to the dreamer like me. In this lovely creek, dashing to the rivers and then to the seas, is the handiwork of a God who knew that we needed a Savior, needed the Light rippling through our lives. From the moment God created our worldly light, he offered light to Noah in a rainbow, to Moses in a burning bush, to Abraham in a vision of the Promised Land, to everyone who looked up at His universe or down into a trout stream.

One of my favorite stories of New York City is that the founders, anticipating the huge numbers of people crowding into the confines of Manhattan Island, decided that two things were essential to everyone: a library and a park. At no charge, people from every segment of society can seek enlightenment in the beautiful New York Public Library and can seek the light of nature in Central Park, both of them places that can inspire, entertain, and offer a peaceful contrast to the frantic pace of the city.

Through all his ranching years, my husband has emphasized the importance of feeding the animals on Christmas morning. After a sustaining breakfast, we always bundle up and chore, sometimes just feeding the horses on our home place – although awareness of nature's connections reassures that the seeds from the hay and the extra scattered oats will also feed rabbits and other small creatures as well as a variety of birds. Other times we feed large herds of cattle on the ranch where Doug worked until he semi-retired.

On Christmas day 2015, substituting for the new "hands" who usually care for the herd of cattle around the camp twenty miles north of us, we settled in the cold pickup and began the feeding process well before full daylight. As the dawnlight increased, a fairy world emerged. That night a fog had covered this stark land of sagebrush, greasewood and grasses and left it all coated with ice crystals. Now the light coaxed sparkles from every crystal, and the result was breathtaking. Our Creator gave us a world which not only satisfies our needs for daily lives but also surrounds us with beauty so intense that every single leaf, stem and blade illuminated is a source of joy.

That day was not some idyllic piece of life with no troubles. Worry about some challenging family rifts journeyed with us, and the black night had held little rest. Added to that, every aspect of the holiday season brought aching over Josh, who would have enjoyed our family prime rib dinner the previous week end, who welded the pole and hooks in front of our porch for hanging baskets of plants (in this season, Christmas lights), who loved the horses including his horse Tucker grazing near our barn, who always added laughter to our best times. Also, we were both aware of aging, including my neuropathy which made getting my feet really cold a dangerous source of pain.

Then God supplied the sparkles of joy, those bits of reflected light which turned a plain world into wonderland, and the gloom was dispelled. Nature often gives us those sparkles in water, in frost, in mountain slopes, in badlands in the early morning. Where in humankind do we see reflected light? Catch the eye of a happy baby or toddler; watch a volunteer serving soup in a shelter for the homeless; observe the face of a dedicated minister with a passionate message; listen to Pope Francis when he pleads for "the least of these my brethren"; lose yourself in the eyes of a soprano like my late friend sharing "It is Well with My Soul" with a congregation; or step back a moment and really look at the face of a loved one.

Isn't it delightful that our Creator provided us with eyes to take everything in and minds to process it and revere it? What we need to understand is that all of these things are reflected light. Neither we nor the simple grasses are the source of the sparkles. We just need to be open to the hope and the joy offered by the Source of all light.

CHAPTER 42

Wishing on a Star:

Ask and It Shall Be Given

In childhood poems, music, and tradition, we all have heard of gazing at a star and making a wish just as we do with birthday candles or tossing a coin into a well or fountain. Wishes are a good thing; usually, they are a sign that we have been dreaming about things that we would like and accenting the positive in our futures. Sometimes wishes are materialistic, but often they are altruistic or philosophical. The latter should become subjects for prayers, for although God does not grant wishes like a genie, he certainly does listen to our real needs.

The interesting part of this wishing is the star. After thousands of years of wishing for a Messiah, the heavenly sign that He was born was a star. The shepherds saw the star, and the wise men followed it to be led to Bethlehem and the manger. That particular source of light has been studied by many, and famed science writer Arthur C. Clarke wrote a wonderful essay about all of the scientific theories about that star, the most compelling being that it was a supernova. One of Clarke's observations that struck me was that the study of astronomy results in humility. Perhaps the Christmas star can teach us all humility before our God, the God who not only sent the Christmas star to guide people to the Child but sent the Child Himself to guide us back to God.

Is looking toward a source of light and wishing for things that make us happy wrong? Of course not, but much more important is looking toward the Light of the World and making our serious wishes known as we talk to Him. Sharing wishes with Him becomes a source of hope, one of the most important aspects of our Christian life along with faith and love. Faith, hope, and love all intensify the Light of Jesus like a magnifying glass can intensify sun rays to the point of igniting a fire.

Making our wishes known through prayer involves invoking the Holy Spirit's presence in our lives. Pentecost shows us what the power of the Holy Spirit can do when faith, hope, and love are present. Imagine yourself as one of the Disciples in that room, the flame of the Holy Spirit above your head, speaking to people from all over the known world in their own tongues, and remembering Jesus' order in Matthew 28:19 to "Go ye therefore, and teach *all nations, baptizing* them in the name of the Father, and of the Son, and of the Holy Ghost." Do we share our wishes with Jesus in prayer with the true belief that hope and the Holy Spirit can enable us to follow the footsteps of those who taught all nations to love Him?

Imagine yourself walking with Jesus in the most beautiful place you know. What do you do when you walk with a good friend? You talk to each other, of course, perhaps in gratitude for the loveliness of your surroundings, perhaps of your destination, perhaps of the troubles and joys of your life, perhaps of the help you need to cope with pain, grief, or challenges. Talking to Jesus through prayer can involve all of those elements. You can enhance your prayer life by reading the New Testament stories of Him and then picturing yourself walking with the Light of the World while you talk to Him.

Part of the magic of picturing yourself in that way with regularity is that soon you will be actually walking in step with your Lord, sharing your thoughts and heart, and finding the answers you need. Our conversations with Him in prayer are the conversations of two friends walking together, sharing at times the darkness with the knowledge that one friend is carrying the Light which will always hold promise. If you had to walk down a road at midnight, would you choose to be by yourself, or would you choose to be with someone whose lantern would never go out – whose internal light would never even flicker?

Let's return to that star. I mentioned earlier that my husband seeks out a star in the early morning sky and talks to Josh about his feelings and plans for the day. Deep in his heart he wishes his son were by his side. But part of prayerful wishing is a return to "Thy will be done." In return for his wish, he receives assurance that he and Josh will someday be together again, and that assurance empowers his continued walk.

✦ *PART VIII* ✦

FOLLOWING THE LIGHT FORWARD

CHAPTER 43

Forward Thinking for Christians

L ike many Christian people, I started loving Jesus as the Christmas baby and built on that love to a point of overflowing when I really understood Easter. He inspires love because He is Love. We can cite human examples of laying down a life for country or for people loved, but none of those touch our Lord's act of trading His life for the forgiveness of all.

With all of His life and ministry, Jesus inspires our love. He also inspires our respect for what happened because He walked in step with His Father. When God proclaims at Jesus' baptism, "This is my beloved Son, in whom I am well pleased" (Matt 3:17), He is proclaiming that after Jesus' time in the desert and rejection of Satan, He has set His feet on the path His Father walks because of love of us. The one time that Jesus hesitates is in the garden of Gethsemane.

Walking away from the garden into betrayal and death is an act of love, of course. But more important, it is an act of walking in the Light, accepting the path His Father has chosen for Him. In this single act, Jesus teaches us that walking at the speed of Light is not easy, not flower strewn, and definitely not the wide road which people prefer to take. I think of the life of Mother Teresa. Why would any young woman choose to spend her life in the filth and vermin of Calcutta, dealing with hopeless people? What would you and I expect to find in such a place among the dying? Would it be the light of inspiration, the hand of God, and a life so fulfilled that it overflowed into the whole world? Mother Teresa chose to walk along a very narrow path in the "valley of the shadow of death," but at her side was Jesus and all of her being was suffused in Light.

Jesus shows us the way; in fact He is the Way. First, He honors the past, studies the scriptures He is on earth to fulfill, and even stands in His transfiguration with Moses and Elijah. From the time of that wonderful story when His frantic parents are trying to find their son and He is studying with the elders in the temple, Jesus invokes the faith of all of His family line from Ruth and King David and shares it with those around Him. He makes it clear that we need to learn from the past. However, Jesus' walk is strongly in the present, dealing with people and situations and His ministry, whether He is attending a wedding or having supper with friends or feeding a crowd who have come to hear Him.

Among those reading this book are undoubtedly many who wonder how anyone could honor the past. So many of God's children don't grow up in homes like the one created by Mary and Joseph but instead understand Hell long before they grow into adults. Jesus provides the answer to that kind of past when He asks us to "lay our yoke upon Him," to allow Him to share the burden. At that point, and with the help of ministers or counselors or friends, a person can find ways to cope with the past and to learn from it, if only to choose not to follow the ways of those who made it so bad.

The present isn't always easy, either, and it wasn't for Jesus. When He weeps over Jerusalem, He experiences one of those present moments when everything we do seems futile and bleak. Further, imagine experiencing Jesus' present experiences from Gethsemane to Easter morning, with whipping, mocking, the horrendous experience of carrying the cross to Golgotha, the Crucifixion, and the descent into Hell to deal with the sins of the whole world. Anyone who experiences physical, mental, emotional and spiritual agony can identify with Jesus' experiences. We also need to understand that from the time of His mortal death until He rose again, Jesus had to allow His light, the light of God, to be temporarily extinguished. In the darkness of the grave, in the darkness of Hell, He atoned for all of our sins so that He could return in the Resurrection as the Savior of the world. The experience of Jesus from death to Resurrection reminds us that we cannot get to our future hope without traveling in the present, absorbing the reality of daily living, but always with the hope of eternity with Him.

CHAPTER 44

Forward Thinking
Despite Present Darkness

How do you get healed from a horrible past or cope with a horrible present? Jesus gives us the answer in His focus, which is always on the future. His footsteps in the present, walking at the speed of Light, are aimed toward the future, toward the day when He can return to the Father knowing that He has atoned for all sins and given Peter and the others the inspiration to continue in the Light and establish His church. Many of His words focus on the future, telling us to "watch, for the hour comes," to look for His return.

What do our futures hold? First, we know we are mortal and that every one of our futures includes death, whether it comes early in life like it did for Joshua or late in life like it did for my 97-year-old Poppo. But a Christian death isn't an ending, it is a beginning, not an extinguishing of light but glorifying of Light. Isn't that wonderful? If only we all could approach our deaths knowing that the Light not only is not leaving us but is going to become so much more radiant than our little lamp, "this little light of mine." All of the reports of bright light in near-death experiences remind us that the

Light waiting for us will be brighter than the most beautiful sunrise we have ever experienced.

However, even though we live as Christians knowing that sometime we will die and go to Heaven to live permanently in the Light, Jesus has taught us that our future focus cannot be entirely on the end of our lives. Walking at the speed of Light is something we need to do in every journey within our lives. When some high schoolers leave their graduation to the tune of "My future's so bright I gotta wear shades," they are experiencing the kind of future hope which illuminates life. As long as we make choices based on the will of God, with prayer and strong understanding of our own abilities and possibilities, we can have years of success and happiness. The world needs our contributions, our relationships, our Christian witness to the Good News and service to others. It also needs our special talents.

When Roseanne was undergoing treatment for cancer, I wrote this poem for her:

Night Journey

Eyes bright, the lonely car and I
bear down upon the dark unknown,
secure only in our tiny field of light,
an oasis in the barren gloom.
Even the ghostly badlands offer
hazy relief from the empty darkness,
and occasionally another pair of eyes
blinks at us, then passes on.

Sometimes in the untouchable distance
a town appears like a handful
of stars scattered on the prairies,
enlightening a piece of the void.
We approach and bask momentarily in
its glow and the warmth of habitation,
even if the people are silent, asleep
in their own individual oblivion.

In a moment the town is gone,
just a fleeting rearview vision
fading into the blackness again
and with its disappearance, deepening
the despair of our isolation.
Even destination is a doubtful goal
with no horizon to define the future.

Yet after so many hours of night,
a faint glow begins in the eastern sky
and slowly eyes and heart find hope.
Somehow this gloom is not destiny
but only a condition for coping with
as we move from darkness into dawn.

--C.J. HESER, APRIL 1995

What happens during "Night Journey"? Cancer patients – or anyone else on a journey which involves the lonely feeling of trouble within our individual bodies or minds -- confront darkness, fear, even ghosts. We occasionally meet someone else on the same road, but that can be impersonal and momentary. We are aware that community is still around us, but like the people sleeping in the town the car passes, members of the community can be wrapped up in their own lives or asleep to our needs. However, the journey becomes worthwhile when we start to perceive a hint of hope – and notice that the hope comes when the light starts to permeate the darkness. Over that horizon is Jesus, waiting for us to open our eyes and know that He is Lord, giving us promise that our journey always ends in Him, in the Light. Is it any wonder that every report of a near-death experience includes a bright light? He told us He was the Light of the World, the Light shining in the darkness, an ever-present hope in the face of despair.

CHAPTER 45

Honesty about Past and Present

D oes all of this talk about the future mean that we Christians
should totally discard the past? Of course not, partly because
it cannot be done and partly because preserving the right
parts of the past teaches us lessons which affect our present and
future. One major aspect of dealing with the past is forgiveness. Of
course, we need help to achieve forgiveness in many situations, but
forgiveness is essential to our Christian faith and wholesome lives. If
we cannot forgive, we need to seek help from a pastor or a counselor
or psychiatrist who respects our Christian beliefs. Lack of forgiveness,
not only of others but of ourselves, is one of the major blocks of the
Light of Jesus in our lives.

I have told you Roseanne's story, but there is another chapter.
The principal who had ended her career was ousted from the system
just a couple of years later. Then, while Roseanne was in remission
from cancer but struggling with depression and alcoholism, the
principal died. I received a call from her one night and listened in
anguish as she cried and revealed recurring dreams of fighting with
the principal. She blurted, "I'm fighting with a dead man," to which
I replied, "And the only one hurting is you." We talked for hours and
her anguish subsided, but it did not end entirely. On her deathbed

she finally told me that she had reached being able to forgive the principal with Jesus' help. She was ready to go toward the Light.

Despite great difficulty, we often can forgive, but forgetting is a different matter. For our own mental and spiritual well-being, it is important that we forget to the point of dismissing the wrongs or situations from our daily thoughts. However, sometimes total forgetting may not be the best idea even if it could be accomplished. If we forget, we cannot learn from our mistakes. The past can enhance both our present and our future, whether it contains a lesson learned or whether it contains great joy. As I mentioned with Josh's funeral, photographs and stories from the past can be a great source of comfort and healing. Honoring past experiences literally provides light to help us cherish experiences and people.

However, there are no "good old days" and the past is no place to dwell. Just as the rainbow reminds us of the Great Flood and a major story of Jewish and Christian heritage, it also shines with God's covenant, His promise for the future. We need to see all elements of the past as leading us to our futures. Some people have horrible pasts, dominated by abuse and loss, and I would never smugly advise individuals to just "get over it." Again, such pasts demand help from others, including inspiration from survivors like Maya Angelou and Nelson Mandela and many modern Christian authors and speakers, as well as healing sessions with pastors or other professionals. However, as these models can attest, once those past experiences are healed, they can be the motivation for incredibly deep understanding and devotion. Once the Light radiates into such darkness, it increases exponentially and can shine out into countless other lives.

Just as we honor the past, we need to embrace the present in order to become forward thinkers. I have mentioned my beloved father, and I have to share his favorite quotation, which comes from the Sanskrit:

Look to This Day

Look to this day,
For it is life,
The very life of life.
In its brief course lie all
The realities and verities of existence:
The bliss of growth,
The splendor of action,
The glory of power.
For yesterday is but a dream,
And tomorrow is but a vision,
But today, well lived,
Makes every yesterday a dream of happiness
And every tomorrow a vision of hope.
Look well, therefore, to this day.
Such is the salutation of the dawn.

Today well-lived, then, is the key to the future as long as we are living in company with Jesus. Incidentally, that favorite quotation of my intensely Christian father from a source revered in Hinduism and Buddhism reminds us that God can inspire our Christian walks in many different ways. Reading the Bible is crucial, but if we are open to inspiration for our daily walk, we can find it in many places. It is not a healthy Christian practice to restrict the Light according to personal opinions; instead, we need to fling open the shutters on our houses and let the Light shine in.

CHAPTER 46

A New Look at The Lord's Prayer

M ost Christian denominations accept Jesus' teaching in the Bible that we are to pray as He taught us, giving us the words of The Lord's Prayer in Matthew 6:9-13. Many of us have the prayer memorized, and I have heard criticism that we say it "by rote." My answer is that many prisoners of war can tell you that their mental survival hinged on that prayer and on other scriptures they had memorized as children, a "mantra" which can lift someone out of desperate situations and into God's comforting arms. Memorized prayers fulfill a need just as spontaneous prayers do, and they all should be honored. However, we can gain understanding of our faith by delving deeply with new eyes into this special prayer.

Do you realize that The Lord's Prayer is almost entirely forward-looking? Among His many roles as miracle worker, healer and preacher, Jesus was the ultimate teacher. Throughout the Gospels, He was teaching His Disciples the knowledge and beliefs they would need to establish the church and perpetuate Christian faith after His ascent into Heaven. He also was teaching them and all His followers the nature of the kingdom of Heaven, the will of God, and to pray with a focus on the future of both His kingdom and our lives.

Many scholars and church leaders have studied and commented on The Lord's Prayer. I remember well reading all of Martin Luther's commentary as part of Confirmation, and among the theologians we students read and discussed as part of the Campus Ministry at Eastern Montana College, we found a number of interpretations and thoughts related to The Lord's Prayer. I cannot pretend to a level of knowledge comparable to Luther and other scholars, but I can share the idea that the prayer Jesus taught focuses on the present and future.

~~~~~~

Our Father who art in heaven, hallowed be thy name
(present and future).
Thy kingdom come, thy will be done on earth as it is in
Heaven (future).
Give us this day our daily bread (present).
And forgive us our trespasses as we forgive those who
trespass against us (present and future).
Lead us not into temptation but deliver us from evil
(future).
For thine is the kingdom and the power and the glory
forever and ever (future).

~~~~~~

When you pray The Lord's Prayer and your own prayers, be aware that you are blending present and future in everything you pray. You ask for His presence in your life today and all your tomorrows. You ask for healing, answers, inspiration, guidance – and none of those requests are for this moment only; they are for now and tomorrow and as long as needed. If we sincerely believe what we pray, we are part of that "kingdom come," and the Light of the World is our guide.

Let me add here that two things are always – or almost always – a part of every crucial step that people take in life related to the church. Those two things are candles and The Lord's Prayer, both of them manifestations of light. Candles are given to parents at their child's baptism, lit by a couple to show unity at their wedding, lit for the altars at church services, and present in different ways at funerals and wakes. The Lord's Prayer is prayed by the congregation at each one of these events to show unified belief in God and to ask Him for our mutual needs and guidance. Notice that the connection here is unity, once again that "walking with" for parents and child, newlyweds, church members, and family members who walk together with the coffin or urn at a funeral.

Are we together in the Light and together in our statement of beliefs? Jesus reminds us that not only is He the Light of the World, He is also the "the way, the truth, and the life" (John 14:6). It doesn't get much clearer than that! Furthermore, He lets us know over and over in the Scriptures that He is the ONLY way, truth, and life. If we're going to find our way in this life and the next, know the truth, and have life eternal, it has to be from Him, with Him and in Him. Every candle we light for every major event needs to signify that belief, that dependence and that willingness to do things His way in His time. And every time you pray The Lord's Prayer, remember that you are part of His kingdom come and hopefully His will being done.

CHAPTER 47

Walking at the Speed of Light

Getting practical as we turn our knowledge and beliefs into reality, how can we travel at the speed of Light, joining our journey with the Light of the World? First, we can take His hand. I love His invitation: "Take my yoke upon you and learn from me, for I am gentle and humble of heart, and you will find rest for your souls" (Matthew 11:29). The concept of the yoke that fits over two oxen to encourage them to pull the load together is part of the inspiration for the central idea of this book: walking with Jesus, walking at His speed, and finding ourselves doing so with ease.

If we accept that offer and lean on Him, letting Him set the pace, we find that traveling at the speed of Light is something we can do. Are we going to stumble, even fall at times? Of course, because we are human – but He understands that better than anyone else can, and He'll pick us up and get us back in stride. After all, we are yoked with the Light of the World and learning from Him, finding rest and ease and confidence. Those of us into exercising know that walking increases endorphins, wonderful little natural painkillers which improve the sense of well-being.

Despite the rich promise of imagining ourselves walking in beauty with our Savior, we do not, as the old hymn says, "come to the garden alone," nor will we have an experience which "none other has ever known." Christianity is a communal religion, one where we share creeds of beliefs and worship together. If we walk in step with Jesus, we find ourselves in great company with other believers who have discovered the value and necessity of walking in the Light. We share the scriptures, talk to each other about our faith, and pray in confidence to Him.

One of the loveliest stories in the Gospels is the story of two men walking on the road to Emmaus and suddenly finding Jesus walking with them. They learn from Him during their walk, and then at supper they discover who He is when He breaks bread with them. Can you imagine those men and their further walks? They will always know how to walk with Jesus, and they will always have each other to talk with about their experience and their journey. We, too, can find mentors and friends who walk with Jesus and who want to share the journey. Often they are in our church communities, often in our families, sometimes in our work places, sometimes in unexpected places. Sometimes they are in the pages of a book.

For example, among the many people who have given me inspiration in my walk with Jesus is Norman Vincent Peale in his classic *The Power of Positive Thinking*. He so obviously walked in step, in the Light, and shared the results of his thoughts on that walk with people like me. Peale is no Army sergeant, but he definitely can get his readers to fall into step with him and his Lord. My favorite quotation (among many) from Peale is, "There is a real magic in enthusiasm. It spells the difference between mediocrity and accomplishment." Enthusiasm seems to come naturally to me, but any time it flags I think of Peale and grasp that magic again.

Once you begin walking at the speed of Light, you can find further illumination for your path from many sources. With Jesus shedding His Light into every aspect of your life, you will be able to discern which sources and choices enhance that Light and which threaten to obscure it. Warning signals will sound like a video game if you veer close to things which are not healthy for your spiritual journey. After all, you are walking beside the Lord who took on the Devil in the wilderness and won! Need help? Ask Him and ask other believers to pray for you for strength and then rely on their strength and prayers as you resume your walk and find your sense of balance and peace again.

I leave you with a blessing. "May the blessed Lord Jesus, Light of the World, embrace you every day of your journey, granting you His grace, surrounding you with His love, and guiding your feet in His way. And may the power of God and the indwelling of the Holy Spirit be with you all the days of your life on earth and all through eternity. Amen.

ABOUT THE AUTHOR

Cheryl J. Heser holds a B.A. in American and English Literature from Eastern Montana College and an M.F.A. in Creative Writing from Lindenwood University. Her life history includes church service in several denominations and extensive Bible study, a solid marriage and raising three children. She taught high school English, Spanish and journalism and directed a K-12 school library before serving 17 years as Director of Rosebud County Library in Forsyth, Montana. Cheryl was the Montana Library Association's 2014 Sheila Cates Librarian of the Year. She is the composer of *Look to the Mountains: A Lewis & Clark Cantata*; a former newspaper columnist and radio show host; a former living history presenter of *Tea with Dolley Madison;* a frequent public speaker; and a public advocate for the LifeCenter Northwest organ donation center. In addition to writing, Cheryl enjoys frolicking with grandchildren, sharing music with seniors in assisted living and nursing homes, hiking, photography and travel.

Morgan James
Speakers Group

We connect Morgan James published
authors with live and online events
and audiences who will benefit
from their expertise.

Morgan James makes all of our titles available
through the Library for All Charity Organization.

www.LibraryForAll.org

CPSIA information can be obtained
at www.ICGtesting.com
Printed in the USA
BVHW03s2358150818
524697BV00001B/8/P